FOR ARCHBISHOP DESMOND TUTU

Blessed are the peacemakers;

they shall be called the sons and daughters of God...You have heard it said, "An eye for an eye and a tooth for a tooth," but I say to you, offer no violent resistance to one who does evil....Love your enemies and pray for those who persecute you, that you may be sons and daughters of the God who makes his sun rise on the good and the bad and causes rain to fall on the just and the unjust.
MATTHEW 5:9, 38–39, 44–45

When the days for his being taken up were fulfilled, he resolutely determined to journey to Jerusalem, and he sent messengers ahead of him. LUKE 9:51-52

The Lord appointed seventy-two others whom he sent ahead of him in pairs to every town and place he intended to visit. He said to them, "Go on your way. Behold, I am sending you like lambs among wolves. Into whatever house you enter, first say, 'Peace to this household.'" LUKE 10:1-3, 5

I have told you this so that you might have peace in me. In the world you will have trouble, but take courage, I have conquered the world. JOHN 16:33

CONTENTS

INTRODUCTION

AS I GET OLDER AND WATCH THE CRISES IN THE CHURCH and the world get worse, Jesus seems to get greater and greater. I know that sounds simplistic, to say the least, but it has become a source of hope and consolation for me. The more I read the gospel and try to keep my eyes on the peacemaking Jesus, the more I discover that he is far more loving, more truthful, more compassionate, and—especially crucial today—more nonviolent than I ever realized. There is hope, despite all.

The more I wake up to the radical life of Jesus, the more I decide to throw my lot with him all over again. I continually find myself choosing not to follow any politician, celebrity, or religious leader but to keep myself focused on Jesus and follow in his footsteps even though I'm not sure where they lead. Though I do not know the outcome or the end of the journey, I am sure that this conscious focus on the nonviolent Jesus gives my life ever-new meaning and inspires me to continue to work for justice and disarmament in the world, whether or not I'm able to make any difference.

This ever-new discovery of the profound political significance of Jesus' life and teachings comes from reading the four gospels through the lens of Gandhian nonviolence almost every day for over thirty-five years now. Gandhi taught that Jesus was the greatest practitioner of nonviolence, that his teachings offered humanity a new vision for the coming of a new, nonviolent world, and that Jesus' nonviolence demanded practical, political action. Gandhi could not understand how any Christian could support war or violence of any kind, given the track record and teachings of the nonviolent Jesus. Christians are required to put down the sword and seek first the kingdom of God, Gandhi believed. To him, that meant dedicated, committed, active nonviolence in the footsteps of Jesus.

From a Gandhian perspective, the gospel story portrays the nonviolent Jesus as a movement organizer. He's constantly healing people of violence, expelling the demons of violence and war, teaching the way of nonviolence, and announcing the coming of God's kingdom of nonviolence. Gandhi even concluded that "the kingdom of God *is* nonviolence."

Most chapters of the synoptic gospels show Jesus explicitly training his disciples to be nonviolent in every situation so that they will have tools at their disposal when he sends them forth into the world of violence and empire as agents of disarming love and God's reign. He forms them and sends them forth to walk his way of peace and love. In this light, we realize that Jesus is creating a permanent movement of revolutionary nonviolence that he wants to spread to the ends of the earth.

As a movement organizer, Jesus speaks out, teaches, builds a campaign, and takes action. He's a political and spiritual activist. And he's constantly on the move. Jesus is always walking. He doesn't stand still. He never remains in one place for long. He's on a long march from the desert outback of Galilee to the holy city of Jerusalem, where he will confront the empire and its injustice head on, even if that means arrest and execution. He's looking for followers to join his global campaign of active nonviolence. Whoever shows the slightest interest in his mission is immediately invited to join the campaign. "Follow me," he tells anyone who expresses curiosity. He wants his community to grow and his movement to spread far and wide. He wants his movement of nonviolence to keep moving, which means he wants us walking his way of peace.

Jesus is still seeking followers today. He's still building a global campaign of active nonviolence. He's still trying to disarm everyone, heal everyone, confront empire and war, and transform the world to welcome God's kingdom of nonviolence. Given the widespread violence around us and throughout the world, Jesus' movement of creative nonviolence is needed now more than ever. It remains the most important requirement of Christian discipleship today, and perhaps the most neglected.

Every day is a good day to renew our gospel nonviolence and to take another step forward in discipleship to the nonviolent Jesus. But the holy season of Lent offers a particularly good time to return to the nonviolence of Jesus and start again with him down that path. With church members around the world, we can use the forty days of Lent to ponder the nonviolence of Jesus and experiment with it in our own lives as we head toward Holy Week, Holy Thursday, Good Friday, and Easter Sunday.

Lent is a time to turn from violence to nonviolence and to become practitioners of gospel nonviolence. We can use these holy days to let Jesus teach us the wisdom of nonviolence, to renounce our own violence and be healed of the culture of war. We can let him disarm our hearts and form us into people of nonviolence. As we renew our nonviolence, we can start again on the journey of discipleship on the way of the cross and the resurrection to do our part for justice, disarmament, environmental stewardship, and peace.

Jesus does not want us just to talk the talk, but to walk his walk. His walk takes us on a very particular way, the narrow path of nonviolence. Indeed, as the Gospel of John announces, Jesus embodies this narrow path of nonviolence. He is the Way we must walk. Lent is a good time to start walking again in the footsteps of the nonviolent Jesus.

During the first three centuries, the early church insisted on the nonviolence of Jesus. It became a requirement for baptism, a hallmark of the faith. If you were baptized as a follower of Jesus, you took up the path of nonviolence, which meant you faced the real possibility of martyrdom at the hands of Roman soldiers. They named their faith "the Way." In a world of empire and permanent war, Jesus was the Way. His life was a path, and we his followers walked that path knowing that it meant walking against the entire culture of violence, the empire of permanent warfare, toward a whole new realm of peace, love, compassion, and justice, where there is no more violence, war, killing, or death.

We walk that way of nonviolence because our first priority is to follow the nonviolent Jesus. We want to follow the nonviolent Jesus and do what he says, even if we don't fully understand it. We will try to follow him along the way of the cross, to resist systemic injustice and war, to enter the new life of resurrection and the kingdom of God, and to inspire many others to join us on the journey.

Our world of war, poverty, corporate greed, racism, sexism, nuclear weapons, and catastrophic climate change demonstrates the total failure of violence. Its consistent failure shows us how right Jesus was and why we should finally take him at his word and accept his methodology of nonviolence.

We need to start again and take the gospel personally. We can read the stories and teachings of the nonviolent Jesus as if they were directed at us. When we hear them that way, we will find ourselves disarmed, healed, and transformed. As we enter the story of the gospels, we let the nonviolent Jesus form us, teach us, train us, that we too might walk his path of active nonviolence. He wants us to heal every one we know of violence, to expel the demons of war and empire, and to announce the coming of God's reign of nonviolence through our political work to end war, poverty, and environmental destruction. He wants us to practice what he preaches, to learn his lessons, and to take up where he left off.

Jesus wants to send us out as missionaries of peace and non-violence into the world of war and violence. For that, we need training and preparation. We need a daily practice of quiet meditation, the support of community and friends, and a long-haul view of salvation history. Renewed by the nonviolence of Jesus, we can take a step forward, walk the way of nonviolence, and offer sisters and brothers everywhere his gift of peace.

The meditations in this book focus on the journey of the nonviolent Jesus from Galilee to Jerusalem, where he engages the culture of violence and empire and undergoes arrest and execution. We watch as he decides to face Jerusalem, sends emissaries ahead of him on the mission of peace, trains his followers to practice nonviolence with him as he embarks on his campaign, and enters Jerusalem on a donkey as a symbol of a nonviolent king. Even through his last supper, betrayal, abandonment, arrest, torture, and execution, we notice his meticulous nonviolence.

Then, when he rises from the dead, he stuns us by his usual nonviolence. Without a trace of anger, vengeance, resentment, or bitterness, he gives us his gift of peace and sends us back to Galilee to start our own journey to our own Jerusalems. He sends us forth to walk the way of nonviolence in his footsteps. As we walk with him, we will be invited to take new steps in our own lives to put his way of nonviolence into practice for ourselves.

This little book is intended for prayerful personal reflection and small group discussion. It can be used at any time of year, but is recommended for use during the holy season of Lent as a time to restart the journey, to get us walking the way of nonviolence once again. Lent is a time of conversion, what the gospels call *metanoia*, which means turning from the direction we are going toward the opposite direction. Instead of walking the path of violence, war, greed, nationalism, and empire, we turn around and walk in the opposite direction, on the narrow way of peace, love, compassion, prayer, humility, grace, and nonviolence. We follow the nonviolent Jesus as the highest priority in our lives, and we become, in the process, more and more like him—practitioners of peace, love, and nonviolence. That is what he wants of us.

At the end of each chapter, I have added a few questions for personal reflection. I recommend that you keep a lenten journal and write down your reflections on these questions, that you might understand better your own gospel journey on the road to peace and your next step.

As we ponder his journey of nonviolence in these meditations, I invite us to take time each day in daily meditation, mindful peace, gospel reading, and some experimentation with gospel nonviolence. I invite us to turn from the world's way of violence, to renounce our own violence, to cultivate inner nonviolence, and to walk anew the path of nonviolence that Jesus has set out before us.

As we walk with Jesus on this way of nonviolence, we will be more and more disarmed and transformed to become full-time practitioners of gospel nonviolence, mature disciples, and apostles. Like Gandhi, Dr. King, Rosa Parks, Oscar Romero, and Dorothy Day, we will become gospel peacemakers to a world of violence and war and fulfill our vocations to be the sons and daughters of the God of peace.

May these meditations encourage you to walk the way of the nonviolent Jesus and herald anew the coming of God's reign of nonviolence.

John Dear

THE TURNING POINT

JESUS APPEARS ON THE SCENE IN NOWHERESVILLE, Palestine, on the outskirts of the brutal Roman Empire, and announces that "the kingdom of God is at hand." His proclamation is a bombshell or, better, a spiritual explosion of peace, hope, love, and nonviolence. Out of nowhere comes the answer to every question—nonviolent love is the way forward—but it comes with a price: it has to be practiced. Sign up now and get an all-expense-paid pass into an eternity of peace. The kingdom of God is at hand. Come on in, the water's fine!

Almost immediately, our nonviolent messenger calls the poor and disenfranchised around him to follow him as his disciples. In light of his loving charisma, they drop everything and follow him. Overnight, he creates a community of prayer, hope, friendship, political awareness, and nonviolent action. He builds a community of peace around him and then hits the road.

In other words, he sets off walking.

Jesus and his peace community go everywhere. And everywhere they walk, they announce the good news of the coming of God's reign of nonviolence. Jesus heals people of their violence, expels the demons of empire, and invites everyone to welcome God's reign of nonviolence and peace. Within a fortnight, he becomes wildly famous. His presence is transforming, healing, electrifying. Even creation responds to his peacemaking words. The disciples are both awed and astounded. And completely confused. And yet they keep on walking with him on his way of peace.

This Jesus looks a lot like Gandhi, training his followers to practice *satyagraha* and nonviolence, or like Dr. King, training civil rights activists to enter Birmingham, Alabama, and confront Bull Connor's segregated city of racial injustice with active nonviolence. This Jesus becomes Gandhi and Dr. King, if you will permit the convoluted analogy.

But all of a sudden, the story abruptly changes. Jesus announces he's going to Jerusalem. He turns his direction, sets his face toward the holy city, and sets off.

At some point, all of us who claim to be followers of this person need to change direction and set off with him toward the center of government, empire, and religion, with the announcement of God's nonviolent kingdom at hand. Jesus is going to confront the world of systemic injustice head on, and he's taking us with him.

Luke marks the moment in chapter 9, verses 51–52: "When the days for his being taken up were fulfilled, he resolutely determined to journey to Jerusalem, and he sent messengers ahead of him."

With that sentence, the story of Jesus and the implications for every disciple down through the ages take a turn for the worse—or for the better. We no longer walk aimlessly about Galilee, doing good and healing the broken. Now we have a mission. We are marching on a campaign of nonviolence toward the center of systemic evil—the Roman Empire's cooperation with the religious authorities to oppress the people of Palestine—in the holy city of Jerusalem. From now on, we are missioned to confront systemic, institutionalized, global evil.

Jesus walks deliberately to Jerusalem, which means his followers have to do the same, and they know that can only mean trouble. From that moment on, they are terrified.

Why does Jesus go to Jerusalem? The City of David is the center of Judaism, and also the center of commerce. It's where the religious leaders collaborate with the empire and require a heavy payment from the poor if they want to worship God in the Temple. It's the place where the prophets of old were killed by the ruling establishment. Jesus is determined to fulfill the Scriptures and his prophetic vocation, which means that he has to go there, take a stand, and face the music.

In *God and Empire*, Scripture scholar Dominic Crossan puts it this way:

> Jesus went to Jerusalem because that was where his deliberate double demonstration against both imperial injustice and religious collaboration had to be made. It is crucially important, especially in the light of ancient and enduring Christian anti-Judaism, to be quite clear that this double demonstration was not against Judaism as such, not against Jerusalem as such, not against the Temple as such, and not against the high priesthood as such. IT WAS A PROTEST FROM THE LEGAL AND PROPHETIC HEART OF JUDAISM AGAINST JEWISH RELIGIOUS COOPERATION WITH ROMAN IMPERIAL CONTROL. It was, at least for Christian followers of Jesus, then or now, a permanently valid protest demonstration against any capital city's collusion

between conservative religion and imperial violence at any time and in any place. (*GOD AND EMPIRE*, JOHN DOMINIC CROSSAN, HARPERSAN FRANCISCO, 2007, PP. 131-132.)

Think of Gandhi on the salt march, going on a two-month walk to the sea, picking up the illegal salt, inspiring 300 million people, and bringing down British rule over India. Or of Dr. King marching from Selma to Montgomery, bringing down segregation. Luke 9 says Jesus embarked on a deliberate campaign of nonviolence to Jerusalem, that it was well organized and perfectly nonviolent, and that it led to a dramatic public act, resulting in his arrest, torture, and execution by the empire.

"Jerusalem, Jerusalem," he laments along the way, "you who kill the prophets and stone those sent to you, how many times I yearned to gather your children together as a hen gathers her brood under her wings, but you were unwilling!" Jesus wants to shepherd the people of Jerusalem, but they refuse. He will have to try anyway, regardless of the consequences.

So it's onward to Jerusalem.

What does Jesus' journey to Jerusalem mean for us today? If we are going to walk the way with Jesus, we must always be Jerusalem bound. Every follower of Jesus is on a long walk to the center of power, not to attain power, but to stand up and speak truth to power. We walk to our own modern-day Jerusalems, where we too confront systemic injustice, war, and empire, using the power of gospel nonviolence, come what may.

What?! Who wants to do that? That doesn't sound like fun or the feel-good spirituality we're all secretly looking for.

Surely a large part of us winces at this journey. We do not want to go to our own Jerusalems or confront systemic injustice or risk our lives as Jesus did. But life is short, we do want to follow Jesus, we know how severe the crises of violence and injustice are today, and we can rise to the occasion.

Yes, we can walk to Jerusalem with Jesus. We need not be afraid, anxious, or confused. We can take a stand for justice and peace, even in the places of power. We can join the grassroots campaigns of nonviolence that resist systemic injustice and empire and announce God's reign of nonviolence as a new world without war, poverty, nuclear weapons, and environmental destruction.

Most of all, we can trust that we will be greatly blessed, because we walk in the footsteps of the nonviolent Jesus. And so, we walk on!

QUESTIONS FOR PERSONAL REFLECTION AND JOURNALING

- *What does the nonviolence of Jesus mean for you, the church, and the world, and how can you renounce violence more and more and begin to practice Jesus' nonviolence more and more?*

- *How do you walk in the footsteps of the nonviolent Jesus in your day-to-day life and announce that God's reign of peace and nonviolence is at hand?*

- *What does Jesus' turning toward Jerusalem on a public campaign of nonviolence mean for your life and your discipleship? What modern-day Jerusalem do you go to?*

chapter
TWO

THE MISSION

LUKE'S GOSPEL PORTRAYS THE LIFE OF THE NONVIOLENT Jesus as one, long, permanent peace campaign. As he walks through the countryside, he heals the wounded and makes peace. His very presence is disarming. One morning, after the disciples had searched far and wide, they find him alone in a remote place where he has been praying. We must move on "to the other towns," he tells them, "to proclaim the good news of the reign of God, because for this purpose I have been sent" (Luke 4:43).

After he teaches them his way of peace, he then sends them, the twelve apostles, on that same mission, to do the work he has been doing—expelling the demons of imperial violence, healing the victims of violence, and announcing God's reign of nonviolence. Take nothing for the journey, and stay wherever you are welcomed, he instructs them (Luke 9:1–10). They go on their way "proclaiming the good news and curing diseases everywhere." When they return, he takes them off to a quiet place where they too can pray, rest, and reflect on their experience.

Apparently, they did a good job. He was so encouraged by their work, he decides to up the ante and broaden the campaign. When someone approaches and asks to become his follower, he tells him to "go and proclaim the reign of God" (Luke 9:60). That becomes Jesus' definition of a follower.

In Luke 10:1–20, he gathers "seventy-two" unnamed disciples and sends them out in pairs ahead of him to announce God's reign, heal the sick, expel the demons, and invite everyone into his new life of peace. They are missionaries of nonviolence sent into the culture of violence.

Imagine sending thirty-six teams of nonviolence trainers into the war-torn countryside to invite people out of war, poverty, and empire into the new life of loving nonviolence!

Jesus is not just a community organizer or a movement builder; he's a nonviolent general who commands a nonviolent army. Instead of waging war, he wages peace. He sends them out to disarm everyone, dismantle the empire, and lead humanity into the peace of God's reign. He mobilizes an astonishing campaign of active nonviolence, an authentic peace movement—right there on the edge of the brutal empire.

Just as Mahatma Gandhi organized the 1930 Salt March (with seventy-nine trained nonviolent resisters) and Dr. King organized the 1963 Birmingham Campaign (with trained nonviolent high school students), Jesus gives specific instructions for his *satyagraha* campaign.

"Go on your way!" he begins. Note the imperative: *Get going! Go forth and make peace!* In Matthew, he says, "Be wise as serpents and innocent as doves"—which means there are times when we get to "coo," but times when we need to "hiss." Here, he says simply: "Behold, I am sending you like lambs among wolves."

What an image! Jesus sends us into the world of war, greed, and violence as peaceful, gentle, unarmed, nonviolent people. We are to be as vulnerable and harmless as lambs.

But stay with his image. Imagine a little lamb surrounded by a pack of wolves. That's Jesus' description of the peacemaker's life!

What can we expect when we go forth to make peace? To be eaten alive!

This has been my experience. Yes, I've met many nonviolent peacemakers and been well received here and there, but I have also found myself surrounded by a pack of wolves that growl, show their teeth, and seem ready to pounce. Occasionally, they do.

The problem for me and most of us is that we forget our "lamb" nature and think we have to become wolves in order to transform the other wolves. That is not the way of the Good Shepherd, the Lamb of God.

Beware of wolves in sheep's clothing, Jesus says elsewhere. If we undertake this painful mission of peacemaking in a culture of war, we need to be lambs in lambs' clothing, not wolves in sheep's clothing. We need to get rid of the violence within, the roots of war and empire that lurk inside us. Since we are all addicted to violence, perhaps it's better to say: we need to befriend our inner "wolf" and disarm him. We need to participate in our own inner disarmament and cultivate our true nonviolent nature if we are going to enter the culture of violence, meanness, and militarism and offer a real gift of peace and disarmament. The goal, we remember, is that the lion—and the wolf—will lie down with the lamb. Neither kills nor is killed.

The details of the mission are astonishing: Take nothing for the journey—no money, no sack, no sandals—and greet no one on the way. When we remember that he's sending his followers into the Galilean countryside where the Roman death squads roam around, on the prowl to steal, rape, pillage, and kill, then his admonition makes perfect sense. He's organizing an underground movement. His advice is practical. They have to be on alert, ready to go.

Their mission is to proclaim peace, bring peace, make peace, and transform the world into God's peace. "When you enter a house, say: 'Peace to this household,'" he explains. "If a peaceful person lives there, your peace will rest on him...Eat and drink what they serve, and do not move about. Cure the sick and announce the reign of God. Say, 'The reign of God is at hand for you.' If they reject you, shake off the dust from that town, but repeat, 'The reign of God is at hand.' Whoever listens to you, listens to me; whoever rejects you, rejects me and the One who sent me."

Every word should be about peace. When we speak, we engage in the spiritual conversation that "makes for peace." We try to make people feel at peace, to be a peaceful presence in their midst, to affirm their peace, and to lead people deeper into God's peace in their own lives, even in their own homes. By being calm, peaceful, and nonviolent, he suggests, we offer a healing gift.

This gift is needed everywhere today—in every heart, every house, every nation. We are all being ground under the wheels of war, greed, and empire. Worse, we Christians seem hell-bent on a mission of war. North American Christians kill children in Iraq and Afghanistan, use drones to kill people in Pakistan and Yemen, and make nuclear weapons in Los Alamos and Oak Ridge. We have become wolves sent out by the Pentagon into the midst of lambs.

The Galilee seventy-two apparently fulfilled their mission. They returned, we're told, "rejoicing." Not only were they able to help others become more nonviolent and peaceful, they found the experience of peacemaking consoling. They were filled with joy.

If we do God's work of public peacemaking, we learn here, we will be filled with the Holy Spirit of peace and joy. This rings true. Despite the rejection and persecution one can face for denouncing war, greed, and nuclear weapons, this work offers a deep inner joy and spiritual consolation that cannot be found anywhere else.

Jesus' reaction is even more amazing. "I observed Satan fall like lightning from the sky," he tells them. Satan is always a code word, in my mind, for empire. Peace movement-building erodes the culture of war, greed, and empire, then and now. His campaign of nonviolence was the beginning of the end of the Roman Empire.

"Behold, I have given you power," he tells them. "Nothing will harm you...Rejoice because your names are written in heaven." What a promise! We have been given power. Gandhi best understood this teaching. He often told the poor of India that they had more power than the British Empire in all its glory. He described active nonviolence as a power "more powerful than all the weapons of the world combined"—if only we dared to use it. If we claim it, practice it, and live it, we can trust that our survival is already guaranteed. Nothing can truly hurt us. More, we can rejoice because we are known in God's reign of peace.

After affirming the seventy-two, we're told, "at that moment, Jesus rejoiced in the Holy Spirit..." It is one of the only occasions in the four gospels where Jesus is filled with joy. That outcome alone was worth their effort.

One way to understand our lives today on this mission of peace is as an effort to help Jesus rejoice. We do not want to make him sadder, but to help him feel joy because we have fulfilled the mission of peace he sent us on. All those who love and care for Jesus should join this mission of peace and nonviolence to bring him ever-greater joy.

Why do we hear so little today about the Galilee seventy-two? Who were they? What became of them? Why don't we honor and emulate them? Do we want to fulfill the mission of peace, like them, and have our names written in heaven, and make Jesus rejoice? These are good questions to ponder.

Saint Francis took this passage to heart. He saw his life as a long peacemaking mission and tried to send his brothers and sisters out on that mission. Perhaps we need to experiment with this text too and head out into the world with the gift of peace.

Given the horrors of our world and the crises of the institutional church, our nation, and the environment, this gospel story offers a way forward. I think Jesus is still looking to send people on the mission of disarming nonviolence. We might ask ourselves, "How has my life fulfilled that mission of peace? How can I take up this mission of peace today? How is Jesus sending us as nonviolent, peacemaking lambs into the midst of wolves to announce the good news of peace and practice nonviolence, so that we might all dwell together in God's reign of peace?"

We have been given great power. No harm will come to us. The old ways of empire are falling. Our names are being written in heaven.

Rejoice, and get going!

QUESTIONS FOR PERSONAL
REFLECTION AND JOURNALING

- *When did the nonviolent Jesus call me and send me on the mission of peace and nonviolence into the world of war and violence? How can I fulfill this mission for the rest of my life?*

  ....

- *How do I go forth and announce that God's reign of peace and nonviolence is at hand? To those around me and to the whole world?*

  ....

- *How can I be a lamb sent into the midst of wolves and maintain my nonviolence even in the face of violence?*

chapter
THREE

THE GREAT REBUKE

IT ASTONISHES ME TO READ IN THE GOSPEL OF LUKE HOW
Jesus instructs his disciples to love their enemies, be compassionate, welcome children, serve the poor, feed the hungry, and take up the cross—and how the disciples just don't get it. Instead, they ask if they can take up the sword.

Two thousand years later, we still don't get it. We still prefer to take up the sword.

In chapter nine of Luke, for example, we're told how Jesus practices what he preaches by walking toward Jerusalem to confront the empire, and he goes there by walking along the Samaritan border, the hated enemy territory. Jesus loves everyone, and wants to meet everyone—including and especially those labeled as his enemies by the Judeans. Today, this politically incorrect enemy-love would take the form of active love toward the peoples of Iraq, Afghanistan, Pakistan, Palestine, and all those threatened and killed by U.S. forces and weapons.

But in one detail, we learn that a Samaritan village would not welcome Jesus because he was heading toward Jerusalem. They hated the people of Judea and did not practice universal love either. But their hostility infuriated the disciples. When

James and John hear this, they ask Jesus, "Lord, do you want us to call down fire from heaven to consume them?"(Luke 9:54).

How could they even make such a request? Have they misunderstood everything the nonviolent Jesus has taught them? Apparently. Jesus had only recently tried to teach them the wisdom and way of loving nonviolence, yet here they are—ready to kill the enemy. They prefer the teachings of the mighty prophet Elijah, who called down fire from heaven and killed his enemies. That's what they want—a god of war who blesses war-making. That's what we want too.

"Jesus turned and rebuked them, and they journeyed to another village," Luke states (9:55–56).

We're offered the image of a gentle shepherd walking ahead of his flock. They can't keep up with him. He's like a nonviolent hero leading the troops. The key here is that he *turns around and rebukes* James and John. He does not let the possibility of violence, vengeance, or retaliation linger for a moment. He will not tolerate it. Jesus practices tough love and sets a new boundary for us, the boundary of nonviolence. We are free not to kill. We are not allowed to kill. We do not kill people who kill people to show that killing people is wrong. The days of killing, we now know, are over.

The message is clear: put down your weapons, stop your plans to kill, and do not support the big business of war and death. Get rid of your guns. Don't join the military or send your children to the military. Quit working at any military installation, especially the weapons' manufacturers. Renounce war and the ways of retaliation. Learn the methodology of nonviolence. Study Gandhi and Dr. King. Practice nonviolence.

That rebuke was on my mind recently when friends and I returned to Los Alamos, New Mexico, to pray, vigil, and sit in sackcloth and ashes to commemorate the U.S. atomic bombings of Hiroshima and Nagasaki and to protest the continued development of thousands of weapons of mass destruction at the Nuclear Weapons National Laboratories. On that day, I saw how we have surpassed James and John, the would-be fighter-bomber apostles. We can call down fire from heaven whenever we want, and we have, and we continue to do so. It's not "pagans" unleashing this fire from heaven. It's Christians and Catholics. It's those of us who claim to follow the nonviolent Jesus.

If Jesus turned around and rebuked James and John, what would he say to us?

I think we need to hear that great rebuke of Jesus. Nuclear weapons are not the will of the nonviolent Jesus, and it's time to get that through our heads. If we listen, we can hear his voice coming from all sides, from the grassroots movements to church people to the world's poor and bombed. It's a clear rebuke in the face of our war-making. Stop all this war-making, the voice cries out. Stop making bombs. Quit those jobs. Do not prepare for nuclear war. Prepare for nonviolent peace instead.

Yet, after two thousand years, we still want to call down hellfire on our enemies. Can't we build and drop nuclear weapons? we still ask. Don't you want us to fly our unmanned drone bombers over Pakistan, Yemen, and Afghanistan? Can't we please call down hellfire from heaven? Perhaps we think we will convert the nonviolent Jesus to our war-making, or change the mind of the God of peace.

At Los Alamos, where we build the core pit of every nuclear bomb, business is booming. The U.S. government intends to build a state-of-the-art plutonium bomb factory there. Across the nation we are upgrading our nuclear arsenal. Recently, the government approved a budget of some $350 billion to upgrade our entire nuclear arsenal for the next ten years, and the same amount each for two more decades afterwards. That's over $1 trillion more on nuclear weapons—the ultimate hellfire.

That money, to put it mildly, would be better spent elsewhere.

"We are at the crossroads of a nuclear-free world," Nobel Laureate Jody Williams told us during our recent conference at the Santa Fe Convention Center. "It will happen if we all get involved and work for it." She told stories from her Vermont childhood, how she and her classmates had to hide under their school desks to be prepared in case a nuclear bomb was dropped on her school. But those days of hiding and accepting the possibility of nuclear war are over, she said. We all have to stand up and speak out for nuclear disarmament.

Nobel Laureate Mairead Maguire called us to be people of nonviolence, to take Jesus seriously and obey his teachings of universal love and peace. She spoke of the late Fr. George Zabelka, one of the chaplains for the Enola Gay, who blessed the men as they flew off to drop the bomb on Hiroshima, and told them, on their return, "Congratulations on a job well done!" Years later, he went to Hiroshima, learned about the suffering caused by nuclear bombs, and converted to gospel nonviolence. He heard the rebuke of Jesus and spent the remainder of his life repenting and teaching the lessons of peace.

"The American people need to say they are sorry to the people of Japan for dropping atomic bombs on them," Mairead told us. "If you do not say you're sorry, then you end up repeating your violence...Violence is a preventable disease. We need to teach each other nonviolence."

After the conference, nearly three hundred of us lined Trinity Drive in Los Alamos and sat down in sackcloth and ashes for thirty minutes of silent prayer in the hot sun. We were repenting of our complicity with the culture of war and the mortal sin of nuclear weapons and begging the God of peace for a miracle of nuclear disarmament. We were trying to hear that rebuke of Jesus and to respond appropriately.

At the closing rally by Ashley Pond, Mairead and Jody called us to push the U.S. government to get rid of nuclear weapons. Write letters, make calls, contact the media, organize events, and do what you can, they said. "As citizens, we don't just have rights," Jody says. "We have responsibilities. Change happens not because you want it to happen, but because you make it happen."

As we remember Hiroshima and Nagasaki and ponder the horrific violence of our world, my hope and prayer is that church people everywhere will hear again the loving rebuke of Jesus, take it to heart, put down our weapons, practice nonviolence, and follow him where he wants to lead us—into the greener pastures of peace, the new life of nonviolence.

QUESTIONS FOR PERSONAL REFLECTION AND JOURNALING

- *How are we like James and John who want to call down hellfire upon our enemies? What violence have we done? How have we supported war, nuclear weapons, drone attacks, and bombing raids?*

- *How would we react to this rebuke by the nonviolent Jesus? How can we begin to love the enemies of our nation more and more, as Jesus calls us?*

- *How can we reject violence once and for always and practice the nonviolence of Jesus, and then help the church locally and globally reject violence and become Jesus' church of nonviolence?*

chapter FOUR

WHENEVER YOU STAND TO PRAY, FORGIVE

THE SAGA OF JESUS CAREENS AND ROLLICKS AS HE FACES off against sinister forces on his way to Jerusalem—not unlike the action thriller *The Bourne Identity*, but without sports cars going airborne in flames. The story begins in a small town on the outskirts of a brutal empire. He gets wise to religious and political corruption and marches through the countryside to gather the marginalized. Together they follow the dangerous trail of money, from Galilee to one of the world's most powerful financial institutions, the Jerusalem Temple, a banking system of such imperial corruption that it fleeces the poor in the name of God.

Jesus arrives at the imposing gates to demand that justice be served. And the powers-that-be fight back, and predictable is the outcome: Jesus suffers arrest, abandonment, trial, imperial condemnation, and legal torture. The surprise comes in his forgiveness of his murderers, in his resurrection, and just as surprising, in the gentle forgiving spirit in which he shows his risen self.

It's only at the end, as we ponder his unconditional forgiveness, that we recognize this crucial teaching of nonviolence every step along the way. He's constantly teaching his friends to forgive everyone who ever hurt them. One can only imagine the blank stares this generated among his followers, but he's consistent throughout. Forgive everyone, and you will be equally forgiven.

Christian discipleship necessitates a few things: creative nonviolence, universal love, peaceable wholeness, gentle mindfulness, and steadfast resistance to injustice. But it requires something more—forgiveness toward those who have rejected us and hurt us.

To reach such gospel heights, we need to practice forgiveness as a daily discipline. Lent is a good time to ritualize forgiveness toward those who have hurt us, to make it a practice that becomes the norm. Only then can we hope to achieve something of the lavish gospel kind—the capacity to forgive even those who kill our loved ones or would kill us, as exhibited at Golgotha.

We recall Peter, who famously asked Jesus just how often should he forgive his brother anyway. (I suspect he had a specific brother in mind: Andrew, a thorn in Peter's side.) He asked: "Should I forgive my brother seven times?" (Matthew 18:21). Peter, no doubt, thought he was being generous. And part of me thinks seven times is indeed generous. Isn't that a little too much, a bit too emotionally exhausting?

Think about it: it's a big deal if we forgive someone who hurts us one time! Peter asks if he even has to forgive up to seven times. That's a lot of forgiving, above and beyond the call of duty.

But Jesus operates out of a deep well of fathomless love and compassion. "Not seven times," he said, "but seventy times seven times...." It brings us up short, knocks the kilter out of our sense of the nature of things. But it is the way of Jesus: unconditional forgiveness, morning, noon, and night—letting go of every trace of rejection, hurt, wounding, rejection, and bitterness.

Many times during his public mimistry, Jesus was mocked, ridiculed, insulted, rejected, and abandoned. Yet every day, he kept going forward. He must have forgiven at least four hundred ninety times a day!

Forgiveness for Jesus was a way of life. It was an ongoing, hourly, minute-by-minute process. He blessed and forgave everyone who hurt him, and so he remained in a spirit of equanimity as he endured constant rejection and hostility. He healed and liberated all those he met, and when people rejected him or hurt him, he forgave and moved on. His daily practice of forgiveness and peaceableness became as natural as breathing to him. When he was crucified and losing his ability to breathe, he gathered his strength to forgive even his killers. Forgiveness was his personal practice.

Anyone who dares to walk in the footsteps of the nonviolent Jesus learns quickly to forgive those who reject us. Like Jesus, we walk into the culture of violence, speak out against war, poverty, and environmental destruction, and announce the coming of God's reign of nonviolence; and so we provoke rejection, harassment, ridicule, and worse. Each hostile response offers an opportunity for us to manifest our nonviolence. It also demands that we forgive those who hurt us. We learn the wisdom of forgiveness—that *not forgiving* those who hurt us is simply too costly for us. It builds up levels of resentment and poison that sooner or later incapacitate us. Forgiveness becomes the only way for us to stay sane, peaceful, and faithful to the journey.

Given the stunning example of Jesus' ongoing forgiveness, the duty to forgive becomes a ritual in our lives. We forgive our parents and siblings, our relatives and neighbors, our classmates and teachers, our politicians and leaders, our presidents and generals, our popes and priests. Name anyone who churns up a dark cloud in your mental sky, and forgive him or her. Forgiveness, like nonviolence, is a whole new way of life.

The injunction to forgive isn't willy-nilly. Just before the authorities haul Jesus away in Mark's version, he says to his disciples: "Whenever you stand to pray, forgive anyone against whom you have a grievance, so that your heavenly God may in turn forgive you your transgressions" (Mark 11:25). Notice the context: every time we enter into prayer. Whenever we turn to God, we begin by forgiving everyone who ever hurt us. As peacemakers who oppose the culture of war, we are constantly being put down and rejected; and so this teaching offers a way out of resentment, anger, hurt, and bitterness. As we monitor our forgiveness and practice daily forgiveness, we receive forgiveness for the violence and rejection of God that we have committed. What goes around comes around. Over time we begin to feel the good effects of this spiritual practice.

As a priest conducting the sacrament of reconciliation, I often remind people that forgiveness is like a basic law of nature. "God forgives you completely," I say to our shared delight. Then I add: "Now be sure to forgive likewise, to forgive everyone who ever hurt you." Many are speechless as the connection dawns on them. Like two rivers converging, God's forgiving them joins with their forgiving others.

Forgiveness, in the end, is eminently practical. Resentment, wounds, grudges, and hurts—they burden only us. Rarely do they burden the ones who hurt us. Practically speaking, it is us that forgiveness heals. Our souls are the ones deepened. Who among us doesn't want that? But the question remains: how? Offense pains us, and people can be cruel. Our memories are long; forgiveness doesn't come easy. How do we do it?

Let me offer three lenten exercises.

The first is to write a list of every person who ever hurt you. Name anyone and everyone—relatives and neighbors, co-workers and colleagues, old friends and recent acquaintances, church members and politicians. Beware, such a list can grow long. (My own, as recounted in my autobiography, *A Persistent Peace*, grew to seventy-five entries before shame got the best of me and I put down the pen.) Your list complete, write a formal prayer. Tell God that you forgive each one; you forgive them by name. Then ask the God of mercy to forgive you yourself. Do this every day during Lent. Train yourself through this exercise to make forgiveness a normal way of life for yourself.

Another exercise: imagine, with all the vividness you can muster, being in the presence of the compassionate, nonviolent, forgiving Jesus. Add to the scene any person you just can't forgive. Tell Jesus the story of woe; tell him of the ineptitude, the injustice, the pain. Be specific. Let it rip. Then sit back and watch carefully how the nonviolent Jesus reacts. Such visualization can be disarming.

This practice was first commended by an activist friend of mine, a frequent visitor to the wrecked regions of Iraq and, having seen the suffering there, a growing hater of George W. Bush. Bush, of course, remains blissfully impervious to any activist's hatred, but as for my friend, the hatred was taking him under. After a few years of inner turmoil, he took up this exercise as his daily practice. In his mind he sat with Jesus—and to the scene he added his disagreeable visitor, George W. Bush. My friend reports his growing wonder as he watched Jesus respond through the eyes of compassion; and then, a greater capacity to forgive emerged. Each time, he learned anew the scandalous heights of God's compassion. The exercise did not stop my friend's efforts to stop the U.S. war on Iraq; rather, it changed the spirit in which he worked for peace. He found himself more peaceful because he had taken another step forward through forgiveness. Along the way, he realized how he too wanted to receive the compassion of Jesus and share it with others.

A third exercise would be to take time each day to forgive even ourselves. Forgiving ourselves also lies within the purview of forgiveness. It is our calling that we should forgive ourselves for all the ways we have hurt ourselves, not accepted ourselves, or not loved ourselves as God loves us. Mercy toward ourselves unleashes mercy toward others.

It's a tall order, this business of forgiveness—not just because of our weakness but because of our culture. Ours is a culture of revenge and retaliation. The forgiveness the Amish community displayed some years ago when a gunman opened fire in a children's classroom seldom finds the light of day in this so-called Christian nation. But it is a hallmark of Jesus' way.

Forgiveness is a path. Interpersonal forgiveness, communal forgiveness, even global forgiveness. Archbishop Desmond Tutu and South Africa set a high standard and broke new ground on national forgiveness. By their "Truth and Reconciliation Commission," they institutionalized forgiveness at a national level. Those who committed the atrocities of the apartheid era aired their murders and tortures publicly, a hard process that set fresh tears flowing. And only then could they appeal for amnesty. Together, the nation took a step forward toward truth, forgiveness, restitution, and reconciliation.

I believe we need such a commission in the U.S.—perhaps

many. One for starters to air the war crimes of Bush, Cheney, Rumsfeld, and Rice. But many other commissions, too: one on the genocides against Native Americans; one on slavery and racism; one on poverty, health care, and homelessness; one on Hiroshima and Nagasaki; one on Vietnam; and one on all the dictators and fascist regimes we have supported, from Duvalier and Somoza to Marcos and the Shah.

We as a people must all look baldly at the truth and take responsibility. Only then can we repent, enact restorative justice, find social healing, forgive, and be forgiven. Otherwise, we will continue to carry the burden of retaliation into future generations.

Sure, we can envision grand plans like this, but we still find it hard to let go of the simplest hurt. The smallest slight pushes us into fits of resentment that can last for decades. Yet imagine Jesus on the cross! From a lifetime of nonviolent practice, from every moment of his own prayer, from centered mindfulness and trust in a loving God, he was able to forgive his murderers and win resurrection. That was the strongest act of courage, bravery, and nonviolence ever, according to Mahatma Gandhi. For you and me, he laid out a rose-strewn path toward a new world of nonviolence, justice, and reconciliation. His thrilling nonviolent saga of struggle and forgiveness is the ultimate human journey, one well worth our energy and effort.

QUESTIONS FOR PERSONAL REFLECTION AND JOURNALING

- *How can you start to practice every day this teaching of Jesus: "Whenever you stand to pray, forgive anyone against whom you have a grievance"?*

- *Notice the shadow side within you that does not want to forgive, that nurtures resentment, hatred, and bitterness. How can you let go of this resentment and make forgiveness a daily practice in your life?*

- *What happens when you forgive? How do you feel afterwards? How do you feel after months of daily conscious forgiveness?*

chapter FIVE

THE THINGS THAT MAKE FOR PEACE

RECENTLY, AFTER VISITING OPPRESSED PALESTINIANS IN the southern region of the West Bank, I climbed the Mount of Olives near the Old City of Jerusalem to pray in the beautiful little chapel of Dominus Flevit, which commemorates Jesus' lament over Jerusalem. Behind the little altar, a big window looks out over the Kidron Valley directly at Jerusalem, including the Old Wall and the golden Dome of the Rock mosque. It's a stunning place to pray over Jerusalem and the world.

"Jerusalem, Jerusalem," Jesus cries in Matthew's gospel, "you who kill the prophets and stone those sent to you, how many times I yearned to gather your children together, as a mother hen gathers her young under her wings, but you were unwilling! Behold, your house will be abandoned, desolate. I tell you, you will not see me again until you say, 'Blessed is the One who comes in the name of the Lord!'" (Matthew 23:37–39).

It's one of the most touching scenes in the gospels. He has walked over a hundred miles on a campaign of nonviolence from Galilee to Jerusalem, only to arrive at the Mount of

Olives, see the famous city, and burst into tears because of its collaboration with the Roman Empire in the demonic spirit of war. He weeps because we refuse to learn "the things that make for peace." He could see that its destruction was inevitable: As he drew near, he saw the city and wept over it, saying, "If this day you only knew the things that make for peace—but they are hidden from your eyes" (Luke 19:41–42).

Alas, we too have not learned the things that make for peace. Over the last few decades, we have sent hundreds of thousands of our armed troops to wage war and occupy in Iraq, Afghanistan, Pakistan, Yemen, and Libya, not to mention maintaining our seven hundred thirty military bases around the world. Our economy is collapsing; we cut funding for schools, jobs, housing, health care, and environmental cleanup; but nonetheless, we continue to spend billions—trillions— for warfare and killing. We seem addicted to war. We wage war as if war-making were the way to peace. Indeed, we know well the things that make for war.

As a follower of the nonviolent Jesus, I don't believe in war under any circumstances. There is no cause however noble for which I would ever support the taking of a single life, let alone millions of lives. If we care for democracy, suffering people, and creation, then we need to labor to end war and hunger, heal disease and social stigma, clean up the environment, restore justice, and reconcile peoples.

No, our wars are carefully chosen. They make money; they secure oil; they ensure weapons sales; they bring military hegemony; they keep the generals rich and in power. But they also guarantee our own further economic collapse and destruction. And, of course, they lead us far from the God of peace. War and its metaphors always lead to death and the loss of one's soul.

I can imagine Jesus lamenting today: *America, America, you who bomb children, execute people, and prepare nuclear warfare, how many times I yearned to gather your children together...but you were unwilling. If this day you only knew the things that make for peace!*

What to do? What is the Christian response? Jerusalem is now Washington, DC. Indeed, Jerusalem has become the world. At some point, each of us has to lament and weep with Jesus over our inability to learn the things that make for peace.

I recommend spending time in prayer trying to hear and comfort the nonviolent Jesus. As we approach Holy Week, imagine sitting with Jesus on the Mount of Olives. See him weep. Hear him lament our rejection of the things that make for peace. Listen to him; hold him; comfort him. What does he say to you in that moment? How do you react? And most of all, notice whether or not you want to learn the things that make for peace.

The challenge is to side with this nonviolent Jesus who knows the things that make for peace and, therefore, to learn from him the things that make for peace. As followers of the nonviolent Jesus, we want to do what others were not able to do—to learn the things that make for peace.

As we determine to spend our lives walking the way of nonviolence with Jesus, we choose to become people who do not reject the things that make for peace. We choose to become people who know and learn and live the things that make for peace. That becomes the hallmark of our own lives.

What are the things that make for peace? The Sermon on the Mount catalogues a long to-do list for peace, love, nonviolence, and justice. Peace comes through regular prayer and trust in the God of peace. Love for neighbor and enemy. Nonviolent resistance to evil. Compassion for everyone. Forgiveness toward those who have hurt us. Reconciliation with everyone. Justice for the poor. Opening our hearts to God's loving grace. And radical discipleship to the nonviolent Jesus. As we walk this way of nonviolence, Jesus offers peace as his personal gift to us. He calls us to follow him on the path of nonviolence into the world of violence in order to be instruments of his peace.

A few days ago, I spoke to two thousand students in a Catholic high school in New Jersey, and one thousand students in a Christian college in Kentucky, and probably another thousand church folk in-between. Everywhere I go, I hear the same questions, the same lament—*Is* peace possible? Can we stop our nation's wars? How do we change the millions of bishops, priests, and ordinary Catholics who are so gung ho for war? How do we disarm ourselves? Are we doomed to our own violent self-destruction and imperial implosion? Is there any hope?

Certainly we need to spend more time in prayer, more time reading the gospel, more time with the nonviolent Jesus. We need to be on the lookout for any openings, any signs of hope, any breakthroughs of humanity. We need to speak out and take action for peace. We need to practice nonviolence within ourselves, toward all those we meet, and toward the whole world. But we need to stay with the struggle for peace, to organize a grassroots movement of disarmament and justice that will disarm the nations and transform whole societies. This is the work of a lifetime, of all our lifetimes.

"If you want to be hopeful," Daniel Berrigan said long ago, "you have to do hopeful things." I write this in New York City after visiting with Dan, who is well into his 90s. This week, he stood in Times Square with a handful of Catholic Workers and passed out leaflets to passers-by, urging them not to support the U.S. wars in Iraq, Afghanistan, and Libya. Their action coincided with the sentencing of five Plowshares friends—including two priest friends—in Tacoma, Washington, all sent to prison for daring to resist our nuclear arsenal. Their long-term faithfulness to the struggle for peace shows us some of the things that make for peace.

Jesus longs to gather us under his wings, protect us from our violence, and help us grow in peace. He grieves over our addiction to violence and war. But he does not sit on his hands and do nothing. He gets up, walks forward, and takes action.

Just when you and I would give up and say there's no hope, the nonviolent Jesus takes action! He weeps, grieves, mourns, and then goes forward into public nonviolent action for justice and peace. After he wipes away his tears, he walks into the Temple and engages in civil disobedience, an act that will cost him his life. He gives himself for us in the hope that we might finally learn the things that make for peace.

We want to be people who learn the things that make for peace and teach them far and wide. That means we have to learn how to weep with Jesus over the world and then go forward and take action. We grieve over our wars, weapons, corporate greed, injustice, and environmental destruction. And with Jesus, we walk into our own modern-day Jerusalems and act and speak for disarmament, justice, and peace. As we do, we follow in the footsteps of Jesus, keeping our eyes on him, come what may. As we do, we will know and feel in our very beings the peace that can only come from the nonviolent Jesus.

QUESTIONS FOR PERSONAL
REFLECTION AND JOURNALING

- *What are the things that make for peace?*

  ....

- *How seriously do we want to learn from Jesus the things that make for peace? How can we help others learn the things that make for peace?*

  ....

- *How do we weep over the world as Jerusalem, and how can we, like Jesus, then take action for peace for the world?*

chapter SIX

ZECHARIAH'S NONVIOLENT KING

HOLY WEEK OFFERS A STRANGE IMAGE—THE IMAGE OF A nonviolent leader who comes to abolish war once and for all and proclaim peace to the whole world.

Is this really the kind of messiah we want?

Countless church leaders, politicians, and ordinary Catholics pronounce their support for our country, our military, and our wars. Many of us apparently believe in a rich and powerful god who will save us to be rich and powerful, a god of war who will bless our weapons and our wars so that we can kill our enemies, steal their natural resources, and find true security in our weapons. We do not clamor for a nonviolent leader who will help us disarm and create a more just, sustainable world. Perhaps we don't want a nonviolent messiah.

As our politicians cut millions of dollars from social programs for the poor at home and abroad, it is stunning to hear not one mention from them, or the media, about cutting our military budget. Each year, we spend billions for war. In recent years, according to the National Priorities Project, 27.4% of everyone's taxes went for war in Afghanistan. We wage war and continue to spend billions to build and maintain our nuclear weapons and our conventional weapons. It seems we have un-limited money for mass murder but very limited money for real human needs.

The solution to the budget crisis is simple. Shut down our wars. Shut down the Pentagon. Shut down Los Alamos. Shut down the Trident submarine bases, the SAC base, death row, the School of the Americas, all our military bases, and all our weapons manufacturing plants. If we stopped these wars, brought our troops home, and cut our military budget, we would have plenty of money not only to balance the budget, but to improve our schools, fund new jobs, offer free health care to all, build homes, and feed the world's poor. Then, with the money left over, we could educate every American—and every human being on the planet!—in the methodology of nonviolent conflict resolution.

Here, for example, are five U.S. nuclear weapons-related programs that probably violate the U.S.-signed Nuclear Nonproliferation Treaty and that could be cut immediately:

The new CMRR (Plutonium bomb factory) in Los Alamos, NM, estimated to cost $5.86 billion in FY 2012.

The new Uranium Bomb factory in Oak Ridge, TN, estimated to cost $6.5 billion in FY 2012.

The new Uranium Bomb factory in Kansas City, estimated to cost between $1.2 and $3.6 billion.

The Nuclear Warhead Life Extension program which would modify the B61 nuclear bomb, estimated to cost $4 billion.

The Nuclear Warhead Life Extension program, which would design a new warhead to substitute the refurbished W87 warhead, which was originally estimated to cost $26 million.

Instead of cutting the budget for mass murder, we cut services to the poor. If we live and act according to the way of Jesus, then we need to demand an end to war funding and to demand new funding to serve the disenfranchised.

As I travel the country speaking for peace, I meet thousands of people, many actively grieving the direction of our church, our country, and our world. Yet I also meet many people who support war, want to cut programs for the poor, and care little about the world's poor. It makes me wonder what kind of God we worship, what kind of messiah we think we have.

Holy Week starts with a provocative, even shocking, political statement that gets to the heart of our predicament. It begins with a symbolic peace march. The nonviolent Jesus enters Jerusalem by riding in on a donkey! We have heard the story a million times before, but if we scratch the surface, we will find it politically loaded and daring. Jesus is not just tired of walking. He is fulfilling an ancient oracle about the coming of a new "king" of nonviolence, a gentle, humble, meek ruler who would work for the abolition of war and proclaim peace to the whole world.

Jesus' arrival into Jerusalem coincides with the triumphal military entry of the Roman imperial representative, Pontius Pilate. On the other side of the walled city, Pilate rides into Jerusalem on his war chariot and his war horse, with the whole cohort of six hundred Roman soldiers, making a full show of imperial force, power, war, and military triumph.

But here, on the other side of Jerusalem, Jesus rides in on a donkey—meek, humble, gentle, and nonviolent. He is the opposite of the war machine, imperial might, and military power. He comes as a symbol of nonviolent power. He embodies the God of peace. He is a new kind of king—a king of nonviolence. His symbolic act is bold, political street theater at its finest.

We need to understand what he was doing, if we want to

be his followers and live according to his wisdom. To begin, we need to study an obscure verse in the book of the prophet Zechariah. There we read in 9:9–10: "Rejoice heartily, O daughter Zion! Shout for joy, O daughter Jerusalem! See, your king shall come to you; a just savior is he, meek, and riding on an ass, on a colt, the foal of an ass. He shall banish the war chariot from Ephraim, and the war horse from Jerusalem. The warrior's bow shall be banished, and he shall proclaim peace to the nations. His dominion shall be from sea to sea, and from the River to the ends of the earth."

Jesus deliberately, intentionally, consciously, fulfills this obscure oracle of Zechariah. He becomes our nonviolent leader set on the abolition of war and the proclamation of perpetual peace. This is the person we claim to follow, the vision we too must embrace.

According to the gospel, Jesus ordered the disciples to borrow a friend's donkey, and then mounted the donkey and rode into Jerusalem on it. As he approached the city, the people hailed him with palm branches and proclaimed him their "king." To state the obvious: Jesus does not ride a war chariot or a war horse. He intends to banish the war chariot, the war horse, and the warrior's bow. He is the complete opposite of a god of war riding his war horse, as portrayed later, for example, in the Book of Revelation. He proclaims not war but peace. He is a whole new kind of leader, the likes of which the world has never seen. It's as if Jesus had waited his whole existence—an eternity!—to fulfill Zechariah's beautiful image. With this act, he offers humanity a new future: a world without war, a new world of peace.

With this episode alone, Christians are given the image of a nonviolent messiah who renounces war and violence and espouses peace and nonviolence. Anyone who claims to be a follower of this nonviolent messiah must renounce today's equivalent of the war chariot, war horse, and warrior's bow and accept Jesus' proclamation of peace. If we truly hail this nonviolent messiah, we cannot support our nation's wars, weapons, or warriors. We too strive to be meek, gentle, and nonviolent. We too proclaim peace to the nations.

Just because so many priests, ministers, bishops, lay Catholics, and ordinary Christians support war and its deadly consequences does not mean that you and I have to. The nonviolent Jesus who rides into Jerusalem on a donkey has not given up hope. Indeed, he offers himself as a symbol of hope, an image of living nonviolence, a model for true leadership. He wants us to welcome him and do the same. He invites us to join the parade of peace, to follow him on the path of nonviolence, and to welcome his gift of a world without war.

As we begin the holy days of peace during our unholy time of violence and war, I invite everyone to discuss the nonviolence of Jesus with those around them. Ask your relatives, friends, students, teachers, priests, coworkers, and neighbors, especially those who profess to be Christian, about our messiah's scandalous nonviolence, his commands to love enemies and put down the sword, and the political implications for today. Ask people what they think of Jesus' fulfillment of Zechariah's anti-war, pro-peace leader. Ask them if they want to follow a leader of nonviolence or not.

I've been talking about the nonviolence of Jesus every day for the past thirty-five years. Whenever some Catholic or Christian challenges my anti-war stand, I always ask them about Jesus. "What would he say?" I ask. What do you think about his peace teachings? Do you welcome his gift and reign of peace?

"Why do you bring him up?" I inevitably get asked. "What does he have to do with this?"

"Everything," I reply. "You cannot claim to be his follower and support war, violence, or injustice of any kind." Bringing Jesus into these political conversations often sheds new light on our preference for violence and war and opens up the possibility of nonviolence and God's peaceful nature.

As we begin Holy Week, maybe we need to ask, like the bystanders in Jerusalem, "Who is this? What is this guy doing on that donkey? What is his message?" Notice the question in Matthew's version: "The crowds preceding him and those following kept crying out and saying: 'Hosanna to the Son of David. Blessed is the one who comes in the name of the Lord. Hosanna in the highest!' And when he entered Jerusalem the whole city was shaken and asked, 'Who is this?' And the crowds replied, 'This is Jesus the prophet...'" (Matthew 21:8–11).

Most of us today remain like those Jerusalem bystanders. "Who is this Jesus?" we ask at our best moments. But few of us go farther and really try to find out who he is, what he thinks, and what he would have to say to us today.

But we can go farther. The oracle of Zechariah helps a great deal to explain who Jesus is—he is the incarnation of the God of peace, the embodiment of nonviolence, summoning us all to join his campaign, practice his nonviolence, and welcome his reign of peace.

Jesus' nonviolent entry into Jerusalem is detailed in all four gospels (see Mt 21:1–11; Mk 11:1–11; Lk 19:45–48; Jn 12:12–19), along with his subsequent civil disobedience in the Temple. It was clearly a memory of the early church, one that meant a great deal to the community of peace and nonviolence. As we enter Jerusalem with him, we take his message to heart, join his campaign of nonviolence, and do what we can to welcome his reign of peace.

QUESTIONS FOR PERSONAL
REFLECTION AND JOURNALING

- *What does the text from Zechariah 9:9–10 tell us about Jesus, who rides into Jerusalem on a donkey? How is Jesus banishing instruments of war and proclaiming peace to the nations?*

- *Do we want a warlike messiah, or a messiah of peace and nonviolence? What does that mean for our own lives, discipleship, and church?*

- *How would we respond to the question of the crowds: "Who is this riding on a donkey?" Who is Jesus to us and how do we describe him to others?*

chapter
SEVEN

CIVIL DISOBEDIENCE IN THE TEMPLE

MY FRIEND MAIREAD MAGUIRE, THE NOBEL PEACE Laureate from Northern Ireland, advises those who have doubts about the nonviolence of Jesus to spend a quiet afternoon in their local church. Just sit there and look up at a large crucifix, she recommends. Steady meditation on Jesus' passion and death silences all questions. She believes that's the best way to learn his steadfast nonviolence and the spiritual explosion of love and peace that he unleashed.

But we do need to ask: "Why was Jesus killed?" The story has become so warped over time for the benefit of the wealthy, military, ruling elite that we forget that Jesus was executed by the empire as a terrorist. Yes, he was a revolutionary, but he was a nonviolent revolutionary—which makes all the difference.

Did Jesus want to be killed? Of course not! He wanted everyone to welcome God's reign of peace and nonviolence, to adhere to his teachings in the Sermon on the Mount, and to love everyone on earth as a sister and brother. This truth can take us out of the bad theology of sacrifice and atonement that misleads us into thinking that Jesus sacrificed his life for us and so we're off the hook. We don't have to do anything. We're saved, so we can sit back, eat well, live our comfortable lives, and ignore the plight of suffering humanity. Yes, of course, he did sacrifice his life for the human race, in perfect, loving nonviolence, but I don't think he wanted us to kill him, nor should we have wanted him to be killed. I don't think God needed to have his blood in order to forgive us. The mystery of the cross is something much more profound. It's the mystery of God, the love of God, and the nonviolence of God at work in our world of violence and war.

Jesus wants everyone to welcome God's reign of peace and justice for the poor, to love one another and their enemies, to work for justice, serve the poor, worship the God of peace, and resist empire through his way of creative nonviolence. This could have happened if the people of his day had seen the light, rejected violence and empire, and accepted his wisdom of nonviolence. Then Jesus might have lived a long, peaceful life like Buddha, and died of indigestion too.

But instead of accepting the kingdom of God and Jesus' way of nonviolence, we rejected him and killed him. I think Jesus hoped his kingdom and message would be accepted. He didn't want to be killed or martyred. But over time, he realized the inevitable—people do not want his realm of nonviolence, and the systems of war and empire are not going to relinquish their power. Jesus accepted the likely outcome of assassination just as Gandhi, Dr. King, and Archbishop Romero inevitably did too. He read the writing on the wall; he knew that if you speak out against war and empire in a world of war and empire, you will get killed.

The major problem with Mel Gibson's movie *The Passion of the Christ* is that Jesus is portrayed as a random victim of the empire. He's randomly chosen out of the crowd by the religious and political leaders so, in that way, his innocent suffering "saves us from our sins." The dangerous implication of this incorrect telling of the story is, then, that we don't have to do anything. We're all off the hook, so we can sit back, enjoy our first-world comforts, and support our present-day empire.

We need to remember the context. The gospel takes place on the outskirts of a brutal empire. Rebels periodically kill Roman soldiers and organize violent revolution, and the empire retaliates by arresting thousands of men and executing them by crucifying them along the roadways, as a deterrent to the population. The message comes down loud and clear: "Don't mess with the empire! Don't resist us or this will happen to you!" The people are terrorized, subdued, and numbed into acquiescence. Crucifixion is the ultimate deterrent to those who would try to change the world.

Jesus grew up under the Roman Empire. He saw people killed, worked with the poor in the countryside of Galilee, knew their poverty as a direct result of the systematic oppression by the Roman Empire, and understood how religious leaders collaborated with the imperial system of domination to make money and control others. He took action against the empire and announced the coming of God's reign of nonviolence and justice. In such a world, nothing could be more revolutionary. But unlike the violent rebels of his day, Jesus did not use violence. He acted with creative nonviolence, like Gandhi and King, to resist the empire and welcome God's reign of nonviolence.

Luke lists three charges against Jesus: "We found this man misleading our people; he opposes payment of taxes to Caesar; and he maintains that he is the Messiah, a king" (Luke 23:2). The first charge indicted him with inciting revolution. Did he?

Three verses later, Luke emphasizes the point: "He is inciting the people with his teaching throughout all Judea, from Galilee where he began even to here!"(Luke 23:5). He certainly taught them to love enemies, hunger and thirst for justice, become peacemakers, follow the prophets, resist systemic evil nonviolently, and seek not Caesar's reign but the reign of the living God. He clearly urged people not to pay taxes and not even to have any money but instead to trust in God alone. In answer to a question about paying taxes, he once told the religious authorities, "Give to Caesar what is Caesar's but give to God what is God's." As Dorothy Day later explained, "Once you give to God what is God's, there's nothing left for Caesar." Everything belongs to God! And he humbly maintained he was a king, which meant quite decidedly, contrary to media propaganda, Caesar was not a king. He was not God. These practices and proclamations stood against the empire and threatened its power. He was clearly guilty of these charges. Indeed, it's amazing Jesus lived to be as old as he did.

What do these charges against Jesus mean for us who claim to follow him? Do we stand against empire too? Are we willing to face similar charges? Do we urge revolt against the military, corporate, imperial culture? Do we not pay taxes and urge people not to pay taxes? Do we profess allegiance to the kingdom of God and therefore not to the U.S.A.? Do our very lives threaten the structures, systems, and forces of death at work in the world today? Gospel nonviolence is a threat to empire. If we follow the civilly disobedient Jesus, our politics, allegiances, apathy, and complicity will have to change.

The nonviolent Jesus was decidedly not passive. He did not sit under a tree for years on end and practice his breathing. He walked regularly into the face of danger, spoke the truth, resisted empire, and demanded justice. As far as decent, law-abiding, religious people were concerned, he was nothing but trouble. He hung out with the wrong people, healed at the wrong times, visited the wrong places, and said the wrong things. His active nonviolence was dangerous and threatening. He was clearly building a nonviolent movement that had the power to bring down the empire, which, one could argue, in the end, it actually did. Ruling authorities always understand the power of nonviolence better than we do, and Jesus knew that too. He could see that they might crush him but went ahead anyway because he knew that nonviolence always works, that it always bears good fruit, and that it can become contagious and expand into a global movement that topples even empires. He could see, like Gandhi and King, how the politics of nonviolence may lead to crucifixion but also opens the door to resurrection.

It's clear from the basic plot line in Mark, Matthew, and Luke that Jesus organizes the poor and disenfranchised in Galilee and then heads toward Jerusalem on a walking campaign of nonviolence. He enters the city riding on a donkey in a peace march, cases the Temple, and, the next day, engages in peaceful civil disobedience by turning over the tables of the money changers and preventing people from coming and going. After denouncing this "den of robbers" and calling for "a house of prayer," he teaches the crowd the good news of love, compassion, nonviolence, and justice.

In the synoptics, there is no mention of a whip, violence, or animals. The whole event probably takes place in less than sixty seconds. But the crowds might have stayed for hours to listen to the great teacher.

As anyone who has engaged in nonviolent civil disobedience knows, this story demonstrates classic symbolic direct action. It was meticulously nonviolent. That's why we're told he entered the Temple the day before, looked around, and left. He saw what was happening, examined the layout of the place, and thought through his response so that it would be symbolic and perfectly nonviolent.

It's so hard for us to grasp the importance, power, and scale of the Jerusalem Temple. Built by Herod Antipas at the beginning of the century, the Temple was considered a place where God's presence was assured. We have nothing like it today. It combined worship, commerce and government, and was overseen by imperial Rome in order to control the population. And it was not cheap. Everyone was expected to make an annual visit to God in the Temple, but they had to pay to get in. And pay they did. Through the nose.

Every Passover, the faithful made what for many was a long trek to Jerusalem and paid a hefty fee to enter God's sanctuary. The population tripled to over 180,000. Tens of thousands of lambs would be purchased and slaughtered for holy sacrifice. A heavy tax was charged for all of this commerce. In effect, the Temple held a national bank, offered loans, kept track of debts, and changed money for "unclean" sinners so they could pay with "holy" Temple money. The money-changers then added another fee for their service of changing the money. Women, poor people, and other outcasts had to purchase expensive doves so they would be "purified" for worship. The various fees robbed the poor and did so in God's name under the greedy eye of the religious authorities and the Roman Empire. It was an enormous money-making operation.

Anyone who cared about justice or read the prophets would be outraged at such institutionalized injustice. The entire system stole from the poor in the name of God. It is only natural then that Jesus took action to protest this big corporate, imperial, religious rip-off.

As various commentators have noted, Jesus did not merely want lower prices for the poor. He did not seek to reform the Temple. Through his symbolic action, he called for an end to the entire Temple system. With this action, he announced that God was present within every person; present wherever two or three gathered to pray in his name; present in the hungry, sick, or imprisoned; present in the breaking of the bread and the passing of the cup; present everywhere—as he told the woman at the well—in Spirit and in Truth.

Of course, this action and those teachings threatened and outraged the religious authorities. Their economic and political privilege would end if his teachings were adopted, so they had to get rid of him. And fast.

Inevitably, the question comes up, "Yes, but didn't Jesus chase people out of the Temple with a whip? Isn't that violent?"

No, he never used violence against anyone. That is perfectly clear in the synoptic gospels. Only in John's gospel is there mention of a "whip." Written decades after the synoptics, John's gospel changes the entire plotline. John *begins* his gospel with Jesus' nonviolent, direct action in the Temple (2:13-25). As in the other gospels, Jesus is perfectly nonviolent. Indeed, he speaks more about nonviolent love—*agape*—than in all the other gospels combined. With the cleansing of the Temple, John paints Jesus as a prophetic Jeremiah figure. With the mention of the whip, John amps up the drama, then resets the focus on Jesus' impending resurrection.

We're told Jesus made a whip from cords and drove out the oxen, sheep, and doves. Long ago, at the Jesuit School of Theology, my Scripture professor explained that this was the only instance in the entire Bible where that particular obscure Greek word, translated as "whip," was ever used. To get thousands of cattle, sheep, and oxen into this enormous five-story structure, the herders used this particular type of cord to lead the animals up the massive stone walkways into the building. Jesus simply took those ropes, which the cattle, sheep, and oxen would have recognized, to lead the animals outside. Then, he overturned the bankers' tables and launched into his speech.

But didn't he take a rope or a whip and start striking people? My Scripture professor said "No!" That would be entirely inconsistent with the nonviolent Jesus portrayed throughout John's gospel, as well as the synoptics. Jesus was nonviolent from Cana to the cross and back to Galilee. With such spectacular nonviolence, one cannot even imagine Jesus striking the poor animals. Indeed, read this way, Jesus actually saves the animals from their impending execution. He was a nonviolent animal rights' activist too.

This one word has been used to justify countless massacres, crusades, wars, and nuclear weapons. Perhaps we want Jesus to have some trace of violence in order to justify our own violence. We desperately hope he was violent so we can dismiss his teachings and carry on with our silent complicity with the culture of war and nuclear weapons.

Remember John's different agenda. He has a different punch line: "Destroy this Temple and I will raise it up in three days." Jesus is the new temple, and he will rise, John writes. If the climactic action of Jesus' life, in John's version, is the raising of Lazarus, then Jesus' allusion to resurrection here at the start makes sense. In my book *Lazarus, Come Forth!*, I suggested that Lazarus represents the entire human race, which Jesus calls out of the culture of war, empire, and death into the new life of resurrection. With this prophetic action, Jesus points to himself right from the start as "the Resurrection."

Our centuries-long misunderstanding began with El Greco's unhelpful painting, "Christ Cleansing the Temple," which depicts Jesus with a raised arm, grasping a twenty-foot-long whip, ready to strike a group of people, including terrified women.

El Greco was completely wrong. Jesus did not use violence. He never hurt anyone. He never struck anyone. He never killed anyone. But he did not tolerate injustice, greed, hypocrisy, or untruth. He confronted systemic injustice head on, as his disciples Gandhi and King would later do, and gave his life for God's reign of justice and peace.

But he always did so through meticulous nonviolence. Unfortunately, the power of that painting by one of our greatest artists entered the popular mindset and theology and set the myth that Jesus was violent. With that myth let loose, we were able to justify our own violence.

What does Jesus' dramatic, illegal, nonviolent, direct action against systemic injustice mean for us? If he gave his life to confront the injustice in the Temple, what would he want his followers to do in the face of the Pentagon, Los Alamos, the School of the Americas, or our other military facilities? What would he do in the face of global corporations that hurt and threaten millions of low-income people, or the forces that threaten the entire planet by hastening catastrophic climate change? What would he say about the way we have turned the entire world into a den of robbers?

To state the obvious, Jesus would expect his followers to take similar bold, nonviolent action for justice and peace so that we might turn our sanctuaries—and the entire world—into a house of prayer and peace.

QUESTIONS FOR PERSONAL
REFLECTION AND JOURNALING

- *In light of nonviolence, why was Jesus killed? What does his nonviolent civil disobedience in the Temple, to protest systemic injustice in God's name, mean for us as his disciples? How do we nonviolently protest injustice?*

- *If Jesus' nonviolence was active, provocative, and public, how can we too engage in active nonviolence that is provocative and public on behalf of justice and disarmament?*

- *How does Jesus want us to confront the unjust corporate and military systems that have turned our world into "a den of robbers," so that it might become a house of peace and prayer?*

chapter EIGHT

The Eucharist's New Covenant of Nonviolence

IT'S MOST HELPFUL TO PONDER THE ARREST, PASSION, AND death of the nonviolent Jesus in light of our own tumultuous times and personal journeys. In light of his teachings of peace, love, compassion, and nonviolence, the Last Supper takes on rich and hopeful, yet profoundly sad and mysterious, overtones, as well as glorious new political implications.

Just days before, Jesus rode into Jerusalem on a donkey using street theater to fulfill Zechariah's vision of a nonviolent messiah who comes to abolish war and establish a permanent reign of peace. Then he engaged in civil disobedience in the Temple, enraged the authorities, and drew the crowd's rapt attention with his teaching. The whole city was aroused by his public activity. Revolution was in the air; a new movement was stirring up the city; something was happening.

So when Jesus instructs Peter and John to prepare for the Passover meal, the strange details begin to make sense. "Go into the city and there you will see a man carrying a water jar," he tells them. "Follow him and he will take you to a house where you can prepare the Passover meal" (Luke 22:7–11). We know something unusual is afoot, because in those days, of course, men never carried water jars. Only women did that.

Here we get a clue about Jesus' underground movement. Perhaps one of his benefactors had secretly offered to provide the upper room in a kind of "safe house," and arranged this sign so the disciples could prepare the meal, the authorities would not notice, and Jesus would not be arrested. Indeed, Marcus Borg suggests that Jesus did not want to be arrested or killed, and that, had his plan worked, Jesus would have quietly left the city after the Passover and continued on with his teaching journey, perhaps to make another nonviolent "raid" on Jerusalem some other day. His plan might have worked because, oddly enough, Jesus found some safety in the crowds. The authorities did not dare touch him in plain daylight. But then Judas turned on Jesus and helped the authorities arrest Jesus in his secret resting place at night when there were no crowds around.

The synoptic gospels describe the moment of the Passover meal in the upper room. Here's how Luke's version begins:

> "I have eagerly desired to eat this Passover with you
> before I suffer, for I tell you, I shall not eat it again until
> there is fulfillment in the kingdom of God." Then he took
> a cup, gave thanks and said, "Take this and share it among
> yourselves, for I tell you that from this time on, I shall not
> drink until the kingdom of God comes." Then he took the
> bread, said the blessing, broke it, and gave it to them say-
> ing, "This is my body, which will be given for you. Do this
> in memory of me." And likewise the cup, after they had

eaten, saying, "This cup is the new covenant in my blood, which will be shed for you." (LUKE 22:15-20)

When he offers the bread as his body and the cup as his blood, Jesus becomes the Passover meal. As many others have written, he fulfills humanity's exodus out of slavery, symbolically demonstrates what will happen the next day on Calvary, memorializes his own life and witness, and invites us to participate in that paschal mystery by partaking of his very body and blood.

But as I ponder these words and gifts within the context of our world of permanent war and in light of Gandhian and Kingian nonviolence, the Eucharist takes on still another level of meaning: there in the upper room, Jesus reaches the epitome of creative nonviolence. He begins a new covenant with humanity "in my blood, which will be shed for you."

Of course, any mention of a covenant is hugely important. The ancient Hebrew covenant outlines God's promise to protect humanity if humanity promises to be God's people. So here, to my way of thinking, Jesus invents "a new covenant of nonviolence." He will not hurt others or kill others for us, but he is willing to suffer and die for everyone and wants us to do likewise. He wants us all to join his underground movement of transforming nonviolence, his campaign of resistance to injustice, war, and empire. He calls us to give our bodies, our blood, our hearts, our very lives for one another, for suffering humanity, for the reign of God.

When Jesus invites us into his new covenant of nonviolence at the Last Supper, he throws away the old covenant of violence. With this historic, salvific breakthrough, he frees us from the old rules, laws, and ways of violence, war, and empire. He dismisses the ancient fundamentalism that once sanctified violence. Indeed, he rejects any image of divine violence. He does away with every justification of violence. From now on, in his new covenant of nonviolence, we live by a new set of boundaries, based on peace, love, forgiveness, and compassion, and so we dwell in Christ's peace. We behave within the boundaries of nonviolence and so live in God's reign of nonviolence here and now and for all eternity.

At the Last Supper, with this new covenant, Jesus sets humanity on a new path toward peace. The days of violence and killing are formally declared over. A new day has begun. It begins with his unconditional disarmament and invitation to enter the covenant of nonviolence.

Perhaps we don't often think of the Eucharist in light of Gandhi's hermeneutic of nonviolence. I think that's because we're still stuck in the old covenant of violence. Few live this new covenant or teach it or preach it, yet it remains at the center of our faith, at the heart of our weekly worship.

There are so many things Jesus could have said and done. For instance, he could have said: "Break their bodies for me! Shed their blood for me!" That's the kind of violent messiah Peter and the others were hoping for. That's the logic of the old covenant of violence, the logic of the Roman Empire, the U.S. military, and every nation/state throughout history.

But Jesus turns that logic upside down and offers a new covenant of nonviolence, saying: "This is my body broken for you! This is my blood shed for you!" And he follows this profound gift of sacrificial nonviolence with a commandment: "*Do this!*" In other words, "Do the same with your bodies and blood. Don't break the bodies of others; don't shed the blood of others in war. Give your lives nonviolently for others, as I have done for you. This is the best way to remember me."

In this new covenant of nonviolence, we prefer, with Jesus

and the martyrs who followed him, to shed our own blood for others, rather than shed the blood of others. We prefer to accept suffering rather than inflict suffering on others as we struggle for justice and peace. We prefer to die rather than to kill. This is the dynamic that Jesus sets in motion at the Passover meal.

Theoretically, at every Eucharist, we join his campaign of nonviolence and enter his paschal mystery for strength to pursue his vision of a world where no more bodies will be broken and no more blood will be shed. And we pledge to give our lives nonviolently for humanity until that vision comes true.

In this way, as the church teaches, Jesus uses the bread and the cup to reconcile everyone with one another and with God. Through our sharing in his body and blood, and therefore, theoretically, through our sharing in his active nonviolence, we become the body and blood of Christ. We "re-member" him and join his work to disarm and heal the human family.

Unfortunately, many of us who participate in the Eucharist, in Jesus' new covenant of nonviolence, still cling to the old covenant of violence. We want the Eucharist, but not his new covenant of nonviolence. We might believe in transubstantiation, but we're not about to give our lives for peace, love our enemies, or join the paschal way of creative nonviolence.

This gets to the heart of our problems. Do we really want Jesus, his gift, his way, or not?

One way to describe our culture of violence, war, and empire is to call it "anti-eucharistic." War is the ultimate anti-eucharist. It destroys the bodies of our enemies, sheds the blood of our enemies, divides us all, severs any efforts at reconciliation, and kills the body of Christ.

When we partake of Jesus' Eucharist, we take a public stand against the culture of war, violence, and empire, and its anti-eucharist. But it's one or the other. We can't have it both ways. We can't celebrate the Eucharist of Christ's peace and still support the culture's ongoing anti-eucharist of war and destruction.

This Eucharist of nonviolence summons us to renounce the old covenant of violence, accept Jesus' new covenant of nonviolence, and persistently reconcile with every living human being as sister and brother. The Body and Blood of Christ disarms us, heals us, and gives us a peace not of this world. Bound by this new covenant of nonviolence, we are sent forth as peacemakers into the world of permanent war to give our lives in the struggle for justice in his memory. As keepers of the covenant of nonviolence, we espouse a consistent ethic of life, and we resist war, executions, nuclear weapons, corporate greed, environmental destruction, and violence in all its forms. We no longer partake of the anti-eucharist of war and death. We celebrate the Eucharist of peace and life.

I invite us to consider and accept Jesus' new covenant of nonviolence once again and to make it the framework for the rest of our lives.

QUESTIONS FOR PERSONAL REFLECTION AND JOURNALING

- *What does the new covenant offered by Jesus at the Last Supper mean in light of nonviolence? How do we participate in this new covenant of nonviolence whenever we receive communion, and what are its political implications for ourselves, the church, and the world?*

- *How is warfare anti-eucharistic?*

- *How can we offer our bodies and blood nonviolently for others, as Jesus did, and refuse ever again the world's violent ways of killing the bodies and shedding the blood of others?*

chapter NINE

Holy Thursday Friendship and Betrayal

AFTER JESUS OFFERS THE BREAD AND CUP AS HIS BODY AND Blood in a new covenant of nonviolence in the upper room during the Holy Thursday Passover meal, he softly, quietly, solemnly announces that one of the Twelve will betray him.

He can see the handwriting on the wall. The disciples immediately deny that they would do such a thing—and then they break into a nasty fight about which one of them is the greatest. Jesus has only hours left to live, but these arrogant, ignorant churchmen ignore his sufferings and focus on themselves instead.

Two thousand years later, not much has changed. Betrayal, denial, argument, ambition, pride, and abandonment of Jesus seem to be the norm for churchmen.

Rarely do people speak of the betrayal of Jesus and the continuing betrayals of him that occur today, or for that matter, the breakdown of Jesus' community, for clues to the ongoing breakdown of the church today. Given the thirty million people who have left the Catholic Church in the U.S. over the last few decades, and the widespread anger, hostility, dissension, and arguments that tear us apart, I think it wise to look deeply at this painful theme of betrayal.

Of course, Jesus is betrayed by a close friend—Judas Iscariot, a member of his tight inner circle, his core community of peace, love, and nonviolence. One of the psalms even suggests that the messiah's betrayer would be his closest friend. Judas, we're told in John's gospel, held the community purse and regularly stole from it. In Matthew's version, we're told he approached the religious and imperial authorities to inquire about handing Jesus over to them. "What are you willing to give me if I hand him over to you?" he asks (26:15). "They paid him thirty pieces of silver, and from that time on he looked for an opportunity to hand him over," Matthew writes.

"Satan entered him," we're told elsewhere. "Satan" was often a code name for the Roman Empire, that is, the demonic spirit of violence, war, oppression, and death. Some say Judas didn't know what he was doing, but I think he was a greedy agent of the empire who wanted Jesus in the hands of the imperial authorities.

In John's arrest account, Judas arrives with "a large crowd, with swords and clubs, who had come from the chief priests and the elders of the people." The soldiers and authorities expect violence from the Jesus community, and in fact, they got it. Peter takes up the sword to lead the charge and start the killing. If Jesus hadn't commanded Peter to put down the sword, there might have been a bloodbath.

Judas famously identifies Jesus by kissing him. Some say that as Mediterranean men, that's how they greeted one another. Others suggest that Judas had to identify Jesus because none of the authorities and soldiers knew what the famous Jesus looked like. He could have been any one of the Galilean fishermen. He was average looking, very ordinary.

Certainly Judas mocks Jesus by exclaiming—as if Jesus were the emperor—"Hail, rabbi!"

"Judas, are you betraying the Son of Humanity with a kiss?" Jesus sorrowfully asks in Luke's version. Notice: in every version, Jesus discusses the betrayal and responds to it with peace, nonviolence, and sorrowful resignation. "Friend, do what you have come for," he says in Matthew (26:50). Nonviolent to the end, Jesus calls the one who destroys him "friend." He does not write anyone off.

How did Jesus feel being betrayed by his close friend? How did he feel having his community break up and abandon him? What was he thinking as he saw the collapse of everything he worked for? This violent turn of events is shocking, cataclysmic, the ultimate disaster. As Henri Nouwen once said, just as Jesus moves in closer to the disciples, during that intimate moment of communion with his community, he gets betrayed and abandoned. Jesus must have been absolutely devastated. The accounts of his agonizing prayer in Gethsemane show his feelings of absolute despair. He's hurt, scared, sad, depressed, and broken. He relies completely on his beloved God, and through that long prayer, he is able to remain calm, gentle, and nonviolent till the end.

Sometimes I think that every follower of the nonviolent Jesus sooner or later experiences betrayal from the church. And, perhaps, we betray others too. We do not suffer the great mythic betrayal that Jesus underwent, of course, but we do experience small betrayals. As we watch the breakdown of the institutional church and the expansion of our war-making empire, we might ask ourselves: When have we been betrayed?

Who betrayed us and how? How did we respond to the little betrayals we experienced within the church? Have we been as nonviolent as Jesus? More, whom have we betrayed? These are important lenten questions.

As I travel the nation and meet good people everywhere, over and again I hear how good people feel betrayed by church leaders whether in regard to issues of justice and peace, women and gays and lesbians, local parish closings or administrative issues, or Vatican and curia banking scandals. So many feel betrayed. So many are hurt. So many are angry. So many are walking away.

Given the details of the story, I wonder if any Christian's cooperation with the empire is a betrayal of Christ. If Christ is present today in the poor, in the marginalized, in the enemy, in the children of Afghanistan, Palestine, Pakistan, Syria, and Mexico—then any time we support the American empire that oppresses, hurts, and kills the children and people of those lands, we are betraying Christ. Those who supported the U.S. killing of hundreds of thousands of Iraqi children over the last twenty years, through everything from sanctions to war, for example, certainly betrayed, as well as crucified, Christ. That means all of us.

As we recognize and name this national betrayal, we can feel overwhelmed by despair. The only way forward comes by focusing our attention on the nonviolent Jesus. We need to remain calm, peaceful, and nonviolent like him and to pray over this reality, even in agony, that the will of the God of peace be done. That's how the nonviolent Jesus dealt with it. We want to remain centered in that Spirit of peace, love, and nonviolence and faithful to that Spirit for the rest of our lives. This Holy Thursday/Good Friday world offers us the chance to rise to the occasion, so to speak—to remain nonviolent like

Jesus, to forgive like Jesus, and to offer boundless compassion and universal love like Jesus.

"The only way to become wise is through betrayal," poet Robert Bly once said. That's a powerful insight. If we can work through our betrayals as Jesus did—through deep prayer, love, understanding, forgiveness, and mindfulness—we too will discover a new wisdom and a deeper peace. I think we will enter upon a new plane of compassion that we never knew existed.

Perhaps an even greater challenge is the bottom-line requirement that we try not to betray Jesus. We seek to be, to put it clumsily, "non-betrayers," that is, faithful followers of the nonviolent Jesus. Even if everyone else in the world betrays, denies, and abandons him, we want to stay faithful. We want to stay close to the nonviolent Jesus in all our work, in all our struggles with the church and the world, as peacemakers—all the way to the cross, the empty tomb, and back to the upper room. That means we need to resist war, injustice, and empire, every step of the way.

I'm not sure what that looks like because, according to the Gethsemane story, whether we're like Judas who betrays Jesus, or Peter who denies Jesus, or all the male and female disciples who run away from him, sooner or later, we all abandon him. It's only because of his generous nonviolence and forgiveness after his resurrection that the community regroups and takes up where he left off.

There are hundreds of gospel themes to ponder in our Holy Thursday texts—such as peace, love, and unity. I'll mention one other: the gift of friendship. Even as his community breaks down into betrayal, argument, denial, and abandonment, Jesus says with touching warmth that he no longer calls them servants or slaves, but from now on, he calls them "friends." "I want to be your friend," he says.

We have a gentle, loving, nonviolent God who wants to be our friend! He even calls his betrayer "friend." According to the story, everyone rejects that hand of friendship, but nonetheless, it remains offered as an eternal gift.

This Lent, we could ask ourselves: Do we want to be friends with God, with the nonviolent Jesus? What part of us gets frightened by the political implications of eucharistic nonviolence and wants to run away from God? What would it mean to be a friend of Jesus, to keep his new covenant of nonviolence, to understand that friendship in the political context of his impending arrest and execution, to refuse to betray or deny him? As his friends, dare we join his campaign of nonviolent resistance against war and injustice, even if it will disrupt our lives? Can we make friendship with the nonviolent Jesus a hallmark of our lives?

"The kings of the Gentiles lord it over them and those in authority are addressed as 'rulers,' but among you it shall not be so," Jesus teaches the disciples in response to their argument about which one of them is the greatest. "Rather, let the greatest among you be as the youngest, and the leader as the servant...I am among you as the one who serves" (Luke 22:25–27).

We could continue the argument, lord it over others, and betray, deny, and abandon Jesus all over again, but as we ponder Jesus' wise nonviolence, I hope instead we will find new faith, strength, and courage to discover a greater wisdom and become mature Christians who undergo our own modern-day paschal mystery with transforming nonviolence. As we learn to serve selflessly like Jesus and join his underground movement of nonviolent resistance to injustice and war, we may finally let go of our egos, resentments, and fear and accept his hand of friendship.

Why not become a friend of Jesus? Why not give him the

comfort of our friendship? Why not accept his kindness and start now an eternal friendship with the nonviolent Jesus?

Befriending the God of peace, we may yet learn, is the greatest wisdom of all.

QUESTIONS FOR PERSONAL REFLECTION AND JOURNALING

• *How did Jesus feel being betrayed by his close friend? How did he feel about his community breaking up and everyone abandoning him? How did he remain nonviolent?*

• *When have we been betrayed? Who betrayed us and how? How can we remain as nonviolent as Jesus? Whom have we betrayed? How can we live the rest of our lives without betraying, denying, or abandoning Jesus?*

• *Do you want to be a friend of Jesus? What would it mean to make friendship with the nonviolent Jesus the hallmark of the rest of our lives?*

chapter

TEN

Lord, Here Are Two Swords!

AS I TRAVEL AROUND AND SPEAK OF JESUS' WAY OF nonviolence, someone invariably points to a biblical passage purporting to show Jesus waffling on nonviolence. I welcome such questions. If we are to follow Jesus, we need to grapple with these hard passages.

Recently, an earnest Dominican nun raised her hand during our day-long retreat in Adrian, Michigan, and asked: *"What about that text from Luke where Jesus tells the disciples to take up the sword?"*

The key to understanding is to begin, as in geometry, with an axiom. In particular, the one proposed by the Hindu Gandhi. Jesus, he declared, was meticulously nonviolent. He embodied nonviolence; it determined all his actions, from his eating with "sinners" to his confrontation in the Temple.

Luke's gospel, in particular, shows Jesus as meek and gentle, which is to say, nonviolent. From Luke derives the popular image of a kindly Jesus with a lost lamb slung over his shoulders. In this gospel, especially, Jesus sides with the poor, heals the sick, and *feels* for people. For example: "When the Lord saw her, he had compassion for her and said to her, 'Do not weep'" (7:13).

Twice Jesus sends his disciples out on missions of peace and nonviolence. The first time (chapter 9), he sends them to proclaim God's kingdom and to heal the sick. "Take nothing for the journey…," he instructs them. Neither walking stick, nor sack, nor food, nor money. They're to rely solely on God.

The second time (chapter 10), he sends out seventy-two—as "lambs among wolves," a telling image describing the nonviolent journey into the culture of violence and war. Again, they go without provisions, to heal and proclaim God's reign of peace.

But later, Jesus' mood darkens—this after he commits civil disobedience in the Temple. Around the table during the Passover meal he can foresee a bitter end—betrayal by Judas, denial by Peter, abandonment by all. And out he goes to Gethsemane, where in agony he prays. At precisely this terrible moment, he turns to his disciples. "When I sent you forth without a money bag or a sack or sandals, were you in need of anything?"

"No, nothing."

He said to them, "But now, one who has a money bag should take it, and likewise a sack, and one who does not have a sword should sell his cloak and buy one. For I tell you that this scripture must be fulfilled in me, namely, 'He was counted among the wicked'; and indeed, what is written about me is coming to fulfillment."

Then they said, "Lord, here are two swords." But he replied, "It is enough" (Luke 22:35–38).

On the face of it, it sounds as if Jesus has changed his tune. As if he were saying: "Circumstances have changed; I've got us in deep. Time now to take up arms." But this is a naive reading, and it misses a subtle point, one that makes all the difference.

Luke's Jesus is speaking poetically, eschatologically, apocalyptically. Jesus is determined throughout to fulfill the Scriptures, especially the Hebrew Bible's so-called Second Isaiah, where we encounter the Suffering Servant and lofty oracles foretelling the beating of swords into plowshares and the end of the reign of death.

But he knows now that the world cannot understand. Jesus, the embodiment of goodness, will be "counted among the wicked." That is, regarded as a violent threat—an assassin, a destroyer, a fierce revolutionary. We recall that when Jesus was arrested in the garden, he says: "Why do you come at me as if I were a brigand?"

But now the distraught Jesus, just hours before execution, is saying in effect: "Misunderstood as I am, we might as well have a money bag and a sword." Deft writer that Luke is, he takes the misunderstanding to its limits. Even Jesus' disciples misunderstand. They take Jesus literally.

Here's a violent messiah, after all. It's time, fellas, to rise up against Rome. They hear "sword," and off they scurry to look for some.

Proudly they produce two. And Jesus, barely keeping the glimmer of light alive, snaps: "Stop. It's enough!" Or a better translation: "Oh, forget it!" The misunderstanding is complete. The Scriptures foretell it; he resigns himself to it. It is part and parcel of his vocation.

But the gospel doesn't end there. He presses the matter even yet. During the tussle of the arrest, the disciples collectively ask for permission: Can we strike now? And one impetuous disciple (one gospel identifies him as none other than Peter) is in no mood to wait for an answer. He takes a swing and hacks off an ear.

Again a rebuke from Jesus: "Enough! No more of this!"

When the disciples realize that he refuses to take up arms even at this terrible moment, they take to their heels. This nonviolent Jesus is more than they had bargained for.

My friend the late Richard McSorley wrote in his classic book *New Testament Basis for Peacemaking*: "The literal interpretation [of this passage, Luke 22:35–38] is in conflict with the whole context of the gospel and with Jesus' refusal a few hours later to be defended by the sword of Peter."

No twisting or turning of this text can equate Jesus' words with violence or war. Carrying a sword on a journey in those days was not making war or preparing for it. Using a sword to kill others, however, was not in accord with the normal practice of Jesus' disciples.

McSorley suggests that Luke's Jesus is testing his disciples' understanding of nonviolence, and he realizes that they still do not understand. Jesus hopes that they object to the idea, reflecting their understanding of the ways of their master. But, obtuse as they are—a veiled typing of us all—they fail to object. They take him literally.

As for me, questions arise: Why are male disciples attached to the idea of a violent messiah? Why is it so hard for us to understand the nonviolent Jesus? Why do we take the verse about the sword literally, while we refuse to take literally verses that command us not to retaliate, as in "Offer no violent resistance to one who does evil…" or "love your enemies"?

The same misunderstanding of Jesus' nonviolence runs rampant today. We have trailed so far behind him that most Christians and Catholics can scarcely conceive of loving their enemies or putting down the sword. Instead, they vote for war, pay taxes for war, and prayerfully send their young off to kill. Many pro-life Catholics in Los Alamos, near my home base in Santa Fe, New Mexico, make their livings designing and maintaining nuclear weapons. They wield a nuclear sword over us all.

What is so remarkable is that, despite the disciples' and the culture's complete misunderstanding of Jesus' nonviolence, he remained nonviolent to the end. He practiced what he preached. He does not attack them or give up on them. But he does once again rebuke them. "Forget it. No more of this!"

Later he rose and appeared, and, in a spirit of forgiveness alien to us, he called us once again to walk the road of nonviolence, to heal and proclaim God's reign of peace. You, too, will be misunderstood, he explained, perhaps even persecuted, perhaps jailed and killed, but follow me anyway on the path of love and peace. Be nonviolent no matter what—even if no one understands. But remember this, Jesus says: I understand. I know what it's like to be misunderstood by everyone because of nonviolence. Someday in salvation history, everyone else will see the light and understand, so take heart.

In this passage, Jesus tries to wake up the disciples, to tell them that the hour has come and we must flee to the hills. He uses poetic language, perhaps invoking the Exile of old, to alert them to what's coming down. But they are clueless, and so are we. We all still want our swords and guns; we all still believe in war; we all still trust in the myth of salvific, redemptive violence.

"Oh, forget it," Jesus says, shaking his head.

In Michigan, with a twinkle in my eye, I concluded by offering something of a syllogism. If we insist on reading the gospels like fundamentalists, if we insist on taking the text literally because we are dead-set on reserving our "right" to violence—then clearly the passage limits the entire world and the whole human race to only two swords. That's it. Two swords for seven billion people. No guns, no bombs, no nukes. Only two swords to be shared by one and all.

No matter how you read it, the days of killing and war are over.

QUESTIONS FOR PERSONAL REFLECTION AND JOURNALING

- *When push comes to shove, do we really want to be as nonviolent as Jesus? If we dare to become his nonviolent disciples, how can we train ourselves to respond nonviolently to violence and the culture of war?*

  ....

- *How do you react to this interpretation of the passage from Luke (22:35–38) and Jesus' rebuke "It is enough"?*

  ....

- *How is Jesus testing our understanding of his nonviolence these days? How can we prepare during Lent and Holy Week to deepen our understanding of gospel nonviolence and put it more into practice in our daily lives?*

chapter
ELEVEN

Sleeping through Jesus' Prayer in Gethsemane

AFTER THE LAST SUPPER, JESUS GOES TO THE GARDEN OF Gethsemane on the Mount of Olives and prays in agony (Luke 22:39–53). What is he praying? That he might not be arrested and killed! He does not want to be tortured and executed. Who would? But more than that, he prays that he will remain faithful to his loving Father, which means that he might be nonviolent and loving right to the end.

It is the most bitter of challenges: "Take this cup away from me, but not as I will, but as you will." There, in his darkest hour, when there is no escape from the inevitable, he places his trust in the God of peace, the one who first called him "my beloved." He chooses again to be faithful to God, come what may.

The key question of Holy Week is: How did Jesus remain so nonviolent throughout his arrest, abandonment, trials, torture, and execution? Throughout it all, up until his dying breath, Jesus remains perfectly nonviolent, faithful, and loving. Gandhi said that how Jesus faced his trial, execution, and death was the greatest act of nonviolence in history.

How could he or anyone stay so nonviolent through such brutal violence? The answer is because he prayed so intensely in the garden beforehand. He turned to God, centered himself once again in intimate relationship with his beloved God, and surrendered himself all over again to God. He wrestled with God over his situation, brought his desire to God, accepted God's will, and received an inner peace after his prayerful agony.

Every molecule of his being was focused on God and his prayer: "Not my will, but your will be done!" This prayer is first said by his mother, Mary, in the annunciation and then taught by him to the disciples when they pray the Our Father. We are here to do the will of the God of peace, and that means remaining nonviolent, truthful, and loving, come what may, even as we undergo the political consequences of our public work for justice and disarmament.

Since that moment by the Jordan River when he first heard that he was the beloved of God, and through the temptations in the desert and the rejection he faced daily, he lived in intimate relationship with God. Jesus trusted God no matter what. His relationship with his loving Father was the key to his life and to his perfect nonviolence.

Three times in the Garden of Gethsemane, he tells his friends to keep watch with him. This difficult scene in Gethsemane invites us to keep perpetual, contemplative watch with Jesus. As the world becomes Gethsemane and Golgotha, we keep watch. We are people of contemplative nonviolence who pray with Jesus that God's will of peace, love, and truth be done.

Christians are nonviolent contemplatives who watch over the world's injustice and hold vigil with Christ in a prayer for the end of systemic injustice and war. From now on, we sit with the nonviolent Jesus in the garden, remain with him in his agony, keep watch with him as he awaits his arrest and crucifixion, and pray with him for the coming of God's reign of peace.

How do the male disciples respond? They fall sound asleep.

At dinner, they argued about which one of them is the greatest. Peter brags that he would go to jail and die for Jesus. Yet here they are, an hour later, fast asleep, with Jesus praying in agony just a few feet away. After that, Jesus starts calling Peter "Simon," his pre-discipleship name.

The sleeping male disciples symbolize the male church today, sleeping through the agony of Christ in the world. But we cannot condemn the male disciples. All of us prefer to rest comfortably while Christ's agony continues in the plight of the world's poor and oppressed. We sleep tight while others far away, whether in Gaza or Kabul, undergo the empire's terrors.

The male disciples in Gethsemane "could not keep their eyes open." Because their eyes are closed, they remain blind. They have no vision. Likewise, we cannot see because we sleep, even though Christ is in agony only a few feet in front of us. Notice also that the male disciples "did not know what to answer him." They were dumbstruck, unable to speak the truth, afraid to repent and apologize to Jesus. Their failure sums up our own. We too sleep through the agony of Christ. We cannot keep our eyes open to the reality of the world right in front of us, nor do we know what to say, how to answer God or the world's realities.

Jesus wants us to wake up, pray with him, keep watch with him, see what's happening, and know how to respond, just as he did. He wants us to be mindful, centered, peaceful, alert to the realities of the world. He wants us to remain nonviolent just as he did, come what may.

That is the call of Lent: to wake up, keep watch with Christ, remain nonviolent, and pray that we too might do, not our own will, but God's will.

QUESTIONS FOR PERSONAL REFLECTION AND JOURNALING

- *How has the world become Gethsemane and Golgotha? How do we sleep through the agony of the nonviolent Jesus as the male disciples did?*

- *How can we wake up, keep watch with Jesus, remain centered and mindful, and keep vigil for the coming of God's reign of peace?*

- *How can we remain nonviolent for the rest of our lives? How often do we turn to God, do we place God in the center of our lives, do we surrender ourselves to God? How loving, intimate, and faithful is our relationship with the God of peace?*

chapter
TWELVE

THOSE WHO LIVE BY THE SWORD WILL DIE BY THE SWORD

IT'S ONLY IN THE GARDEN OF GETHSEMANE, WHEN JUDAS and those with him arrive to arrest Jesus, that the early community—the disciples of men and women, the first church—finally come to understand Jesus. There they realize just how serious Jesus is about life-giving, loving, steadfast nonviolence.

Lent invites us to the same realization—that Jesus is deadly serious about nonviolence and wants us to commit ourselves to his way. Unlike the first disciples, we know the final outcome and have a better chance to pledge allegiance to him and stay the course with his difficult nonviolence, come what may.

Under the cover of night, in the first act of violence by a disciple, Judas kisses Jesus and betrays him, and the soldiers move in for the arrest. In the second act of violence by a disciple of Jesus, Peter himself takes out a sword, strikes at the high priest's slave, and cuts off his ear.

Jesus will have none of it. "Put back your sword, for those

who take up the sword will surely perish by the sword." These are the last words of Jesus to the church before he was executed, and it's the first time they recognize and understand the depth of his nonviolence.

What do they do? They all run away.

Here's Matthew's version:

> While he was still speaking, Judas, one of the Twelve, arrived, accompanied by a large crowd with swords and clubs, who had come from the chief priests and the elders of the people. His betrayer had arranged a sign with them, saying, "The man I shall kiss is the one; arrest him." Immediately he went over to Jesus and said, "Hail, Rabbi!" and he kissed him. Jesus answered him, "Friend, do what you have come for." Then stepping forward they laid hands on Jesus and arrested him. And behold, one of those who accompanied Jesus put his hand to his sword, drew it, and struck the high priest's servant, cutting off his ear. Then Jesus said, "Put your sword back into its sheath, for all those who take up the sword will perish by the sword. Do you think that I cannot call upon my Father and he will not provide me at this moment with more than twelve legions of angels? But then how would the scriptures be fulfilled which say that it must come to pass in this way?" At that hour Jesus said to the crowds, "Have you come out as against a robber, with swords and clubs to seize me? Day after day I sat teaching in the Temple area, yet you did not arrest me. But all of this has come to pass that the writings of the prophets may be fulfilled." Then all the disciples left him and fled.
> (MATTHEW 26:47-56)

Lent invites us to walk with the nonviolent Jesus on the way of the cross, that is, the way of loving nonviolence and steadfast resistance to systemic injustice. If we do our work and take time to reflect on Jesus' nonviolence and our discipleship to him, we will invariably notice the various ways that we, too, reject his nonviolence and run away from him, just as the first disciples did.

This self-examination is critically important. We need not panic because we feel this way. Instead, such awareness offers new opportunities for prayer, inner disarmament, growing in faith, learning to trust Jesus, and recommitting ourselves to him all over again.

Each Lent, we walk with Jesus from Galilee to Jerusalem, to his civil disobedience in the Temple and arrest in the garden. This journey helps us take new steps forward on the path of nonviolence, that we might not be people who take up the sword or perish by the sword, but people who walk in peace, who work to end the killing and war-making.

But that terrible moment in the Garden of Gethsemane raises particular questions: Where do we find ourselves in this scene? Do we side with the religious and imperial authorities in arresting and condemning this nonviolent revolutionary—and present-day nonviolent revolutionaries? No? Do we sympathize with Peter, who takes up the sword to kill to defend Jesus? Yes? Do we believe with him that killing the soldiers would be justified, that this marks a true "just war"? How do we respond to Jesus' commandment to "put down the sword"? Do we accept Jesus' nonviolence, or, when push comes to shove, do we too run away?

Jesus clearly forbids his disciples from the use of violence to defend him or themselves against the soldiers. He intends to accept the consequences of his way of peace, love, and nonviolence. He rules out violent retaliation, vengeance, killing, and warfare.

In Luke's account, Jesus reprimands the disciples, saying, *"Stop! No more of this!"* (Luke 22:51). But Matthew's version offers a reason for this commandment of nonviolence: *"Those who live by the sword will die by the sword."* Other translations put it this way: *"Those who take up the sword will surely perish by the sword."* With this teaching, Jesus addresses the world's downward cycle of violence and calls us to end it. Violence begets violence, Jesus says, so have nothing to do with violence. Break the cycle of violence with your creative nonviolence.

If every Christian obeyed this teaching, violence would rapidly disappear.

Two thousand years after Gethsemane, however, we still disobey Jesus and participate in the downward spiral of violence. We bomb Afghanistan, execute people in prison, build nuclear weapons, fund warfare around the globe, steal the resources of the world's poor, destroy the earth, and so on. Though others may continue to believe the myth of violence in response to violence, we Christians are commanded to put down the sword, stop the violence, and hear the truth that those who live by the sword die by the sword.

The nonviolent Jesus does not want us to live or die by swords anymore. He wants us to beat our swords into plowshares, feed the hungry, study war no more, and love our enemies. Up until his last breath, he heralds the coming of a new world of nonviolence.

I'm beginning to think that sooner or later every one of us walks away from the nonviolent Jesus. His way goes against everything we have been taught. It sounds naive, foolhardy, and downright scary. It means, like Jesus, we could get killed.

But Jesus has a long-haul view that few grasp. He speaks about trusting in the God of peace and fulfilling the Scriptures. He knows that God is trustworthy, that he will live on, and that we, too, are all headed toward resurrection peace. He accepts the reality of death, but determines that he will not go to his death by inflicting violence. He never takes up the sword. I don't think he had a drop of violence in his being.

This verse from Matthew is worth our reflection. It proposes a new law of nature. It suggests that if we are violent—personally, nationally, and globally—eventually that violence will come back upon us. Does Jesus teach that those who wage war will die by war? Those who bomb people will suffer and die by bombs? Those who use drones to terrorize other nations will one day be terrorized by drones? Those who threaten others and use nuclear weapons on others will one day be threatened and subjected to nuclear weapons? This is the logic of Matthew's gospel, and the history of violence and war bears it out.

Certainly, Jesus could have taken up the sword, but he doesn't. Indeed, he announces that he could call upon twelve legions of angels—24,000 angels!—to appear right at that moment in the Garden of Gethsemane to protect him from the soldiers, like some fantasy scene out of *The Lord of the Rings.* Imagine that! Those arresting Jesus would probably have died of sheer fright. But Jesus does not want to scare anyone or rely on superhuman strength. He remains human, nonviolent, and peaceful—and suffers the consequences of his nonviolent humanity. He is willing to die nonviolently and trusts that he will rise in peace. And he offers this example for us.

John's gospel names Peter as the one who strikes the servant and cuts off his ear. Peter was probably angry that Jesus wouldn't take up the sword in violent self-defense. He simply can't grasp Jesus' cosmic strategy of nonviolence. He sees only passivity.

Why don't we listen to Jesus and obey his teaching about violence? I suppose that we, like Peter, don't know any other way, and we can't believe that Jesus could be right. In the end, we want to live and die by the sword. We can't imagine life or death without our swords—or guns, or bombs, or drones, or nukes. We are stuck in the rut of violence, blind to the illusions of its false security, clueless about the never-ending downward spiral that leads to death, and ignorant about the power and wisdom of nonviolence.

Nonetheless, the gospel insists: Do not live by the sword—personally, nationally, or globally. The sword has become a metaphor for every weapon of war, and Jesus' bottom-line rule remains. No disciple is permitted to take up a gun, to build or drop bombs, or to use any instrument of violence. Get rid of your guns. Quit the military. Live a nonviolent life. Learn the things that make for peace. Love your enemies. Welcome the resurrection gift of peace.

In the midst of these tough teachings, I hear a quiet word of hope. *Yes, those who live by the sword, in the grand scheme of things, will die by the sword. But the opposite is also true: Those who live in love will die in love. Those who live in peace will die in peace. Those who live in compassion will die in compassion. Those who live by mercy will die in mercy. Those who live in nonviolence will die in nonviolence.*

More—if we dare obey Jesus, refuse to take up the sword, and train ourselves to live like him in a spirit of peace, love, and nonviolence, then we will have no need to run away from him! We will not be scared or angry or worried or doubtful. We will want to remain with our nonviolent friend, our Good Shepherd.

If we can live our lives like Jesus, in his spirit of love, peace, and nonviolence, we will go to our deaths in that spirit and share in Jesus' eternal life of love and peace. We will be true to our humanity and fulfill the biblical vision of peace. And we will also stand at the side of the nonviolent Jesus. That is the greatest blessing of all.

Lent invites us to learn Jesus' way of nonviolence, to train ourselves and be ready so that, when push comes to shove, we do not take up the sword, but remain peaceful, nonviolent, and faithful, so that we can be his instruments of peace. As more and more of us accept Jesus' nonviolence and spread his teaching, we can help end the death penalty, stop our wars, abolish our nuclear weapons, and halt the plague of violence that infects us all.

We need not participate in the senseless game of violence anymore. We have seen how the cycle of violence fails time and again. As followers of the nonviolent Jesus, we have a better way.

QUESTIONS FOR PERSONAL REFLECTION AND JOURNALING

- *What part of us wants to strike with a sword as Peter does in Gethsemane? How do we respond to Jesus' last words to the church: "Put down your sword"?*

- *Do we believe Jesus' instruction that violence always leads to further violence—"Those who live by the sword will die by the sword"?*

- *How are we violent, and how do we support the culture of violence and war? How can we stop cooperating with violence and the culture of violence and war and break the descending spiral of violence?*

chapter
THIRTEEN

TRIAL, TORTURE, AND STEADFAST NONVIOLENCE

THE VARIOUS ACCOUNTS OF THE ARREST, TRIALS, condemnation, and torture of Jesus are confusing, which makes them all the more realistic. As someone who has been in court hundreds of times for civil disobedience against war and nuclear weapons, I know how confusing and unjust today's criminal "justice" system is. One can only imagine the horrors that Jesus faced under the imperial and religious rule of Jerusalem.

In Luke's version, for example, he is taken to the house of the high priest, where he is ridiculed, harassed, mocked, and beaten. They blindfold him, strike him, and then demand he point out the one who hit him. Meanwhile, Peter warms his hands by the charcoal fire in the courtyard. As he denies knowing Jesus, he sees Jesus, who is being beaten and mocked, turn and look at him. Peter goes out and weeps.

At daybreak, Jesus is hauled before the Sanhedrin, the ruling body of the religious authorities. They interrogate him and then charge him with blasphemy. Next, he's dragged before Pontius Pilate and before Herod, representatives of the Roman emperor. The religious leaders "stood by and accused him harshly." Herod and his soldiers "treated him contemptuously and mocked him." Pilate offers to release him, but the crowd of people stirred up by the religious authorities demand Jesus' crucifixion, so Pilate orders Jesus to be crucified.

The whole episode is filled with pathos and violence. Here we see the sheer contempt of the world—led by our religious and imperial leaders—toward one who is perfectly loving and nonviolent. We could catalogue the abuse that the nonviolent Jesus suffers—and when we add up the other gospel accounts, it is truly horrifying. But it may be more helpful to ponder the attitude and inner spirit of Jesus as he undergoes this ridicule, abuse, and torture.

Jesus never strikes back. He does not get angry or bitter or retaliate or hint at any sense of vengeance. He is perfectly nonviolent. I think he is completely centered interiorly in absolute prayer with God his beloved Father. As he dies on the cross, he calls out, "Father, forgive them for they know not what they do." That line is one of the most profound statements of nonviolence in history—it reveals the inner spirit of Jesus. He seems to accept his fate, to go passively like a lamb to the slaughter, but that line opens a portal into his heart. Because he focuses on God, he is able to remain centered in perfect, nonviolent love. The tortured, humiliated Jesus probably feels only compassion for them. From his perspective, he could see that they would spend eternity repenting for what they had done. He is eager to forgive. He is also determined to be humble and human. He does not reveal any magic solution or show of violent force. He undergoes torture and execution as mindfully as he can, centered in the love of God, as peaceful and truthful as humanly possible.

In Matthew's version, after Pilate orders Jesus to be scourged and then crucified, the soldiers take him inside the praetorium, the residence of the Roman governor, and, we're told, "gathered the whole cohort around him." The whole cohort usually numbered six hundred soldiers who would have accompanied Pilate to Jerusalem to protect him during the annual Passover days. These soldiers were brutal, drunken, trained terrorists, torturers, and murderers. The thought of six hundred drunken death squad soldiers surrounding the peaceful, gentle, nonviolent Jesus should stop every Christian in our tracks.

This is one of the most important scenes in the Bible, and in the history of nonviolence. Matthew describes this scene before Jesus' crucifixion:

> They stripped off his clothes and threw a scarlet military cloak about him. Weaving a crown out of thorns, they placed it on his head, and a reed in his right hand. And kneeling before him, they mocked him, saying, "Hail, King of the Jews!" They spat upon him and took the reed and kept striking him on the head. And when they had mocked him, they stripped him of the cloak, dressed him in his own clothes, and led him off to crucify him.
> (MATTHEW 27:28-31)

The six hundred soldiers humiliate and mock Jesus as if he were a king, when it's so obvious to them that he's nothing but riffraff from Galilee. Like torturers everywhere, from the U.S.-backed death squads in Guatemala and El Salvador to the U.S. torturers in Abu Graib, Iraq, and Guantanamo Prison, the soldiers take delight in their evildoing. The scene has always convinced me that no one who ever wanted to maintain their basic humanity and decency could ever join any military force ever again.

From the perspective of the God of peace, every military tortures and kills Christ all over again.

Here before the whole cohort stands the true king of non-violence, the embodiment of the God of peace, suffering humiliation and abuse at the hands of the empire. Because God chooses perfect nonviolence and therefore gives us the freedom to love or reject God, God has chosen to remain utterly powerless before the world, even to the point of allowing the nonviolent Jesus to be mocked, abused, tortured, and killed. In doing so, God in Jesus shows us the heights of nonviolence. He shows us how to be human even in the face of the greatest inhumanity. He shows us how to be Godly.

Jesus is stripped of the purple garments, given his clothes back, led through Jerusalem, taken to the garbage dump outside the city walls, and crucified with two men who had murdered Roman soldiers to spark the revolution. Jesus is killed as if he too were a violent revolutionary. So, besides being tortured and executed, he is completely misunderstood. He has been betrayed, denied, and abandoned by all his friends, and no one knows who he is, what he has done, or where he has come from. He undergoes his brutal suffering all alone.

All he has left is the God who first called him "my beloved." I think there on the cross, Jesus turned inward and clung to God as a child to a loving parent, knowing that soon it would be over and he would be with his loving God. It is that faith, trust, and intimate love that enabled Jesus to practice perfect nonviolence unto death. This is the nonviolence he calls us to practice as well. He wants us to go as deep into nonviolence as we can, even until our own deaths, that we might follow him completely and share his friendship and peace.

QUESTIONS FOR PERSONAL
REFLECTION AND JOURNALING

- *How did Jesus remain so nonviolent throughout his trial, torture, and execution?*

- *What does that mean for us as his disciples? How can we deepen our nonviolence, our faith and trust in God, and our compassion for others, even those who would harm us?*

- *What does the scene of the nonviolent Jesus before the six hundred violent Roman soldiers mean for us today? What does it say about the military, warfare, or torture? How can we side with the victims of warfare in the world today, and not the war makers, as we practice gospel nonviolence?*

chapter
FOURTEEN

ATTENDANTS OF THE NONVIOLENT JESUS

THE GOSPEL OF JOHN OFFERS A UNIQUE TESTIMONY TO Jesus as he stands in court before Pontius Pilate, the representative of the Roman Empire. There, in that moment, a few hours before his death, he explains what he is about, which is, the kingdom of God. The distinguishing characteristic of the kingdom of God, he tells Pilate, is nonviolence.

These words sum up the Christian life of peace and nonviolence:

> My kingdom does not belong to this world.
> If my kingdom did belong to this world,
> my attendants would be fighting
> to keep me from being handed over to the Judeans.
> But as it is, my kingdom is not here. (JOHN 18:36)

Here the gospel sets in stark contrast the choice before us: to live as members of Jesus' kingdom of loving nonviolence, or to live as citizens of the kingdoms, nations, and empires of violence and war.

The sole difference between the kingdom of God and the kingdoms of this world, from Rome to America, is nonviolence.

Forgive me for being a broken record about this, but I do not understand how any Christian or Catholic can support war or America's empire in light of such texts. Yet everywhere I go, that's precisely what I hear from Christians and Catholics—we support our nation, its guns, its wars, its violence, its corporate greed, its global military outreach. At best, we want it both ways—Jesus and violence. We want the kingdom of God and the kingdom of America. We want the nonviolent Jesus, and we want to fight to get our way in the world.

The Gospel of John says that we can't have it both ways: it's either the nonviolent Jesus and the nonviolent kingdom of God, OR the violent kingdoms of the world and their ensuing death and destruction. I hear the gospel saying: either we follow the nonviolent Jesus and therefore reject war and empire, practice his creative nonviolence, and do not engage in violence, OR we support our nation, our empire and its wars, reject creative nonviolence, and no longer follow Jesus.

As baptized followers of the nonviolent Jesus, we are not allowed to fight, and so we do not fight or use violence or support war. Case closed.

For me, it's a clear-cut choice: if you want to remain a Christian, you have to become nonviolent and attend to Jesus and his brave nonviolence. You therefore no longer support war or empire.

This verse gives one of the best descriptions of God's reign, the way of Jesus and Christian discipleship in the New Testament. In his kingdom, Jesus explains, there is no fighting, which means there is no violence, no war, no weapons, no killing, and no death. It is a realm of perfect nonviolent love. I think this is very good news, but sadly its pronouncement remains ignored and unknown. We can barely imagine anyone who is nonviolent, much less a world of perfect nonviolence. To speak this way is to be dismissed as idealistic at best. But according to the story, Jesus gave his life announcing this truth of nonviolence, and he modeled it unto his last breath.

It's strange that we rarely hear this text discussed. Why is that? I think it's because we do not want the nonviolence of Jesus. We prefer to fight like everyone else. We know deep down that if this text is true, our violence reveals that we are not "attendants" of the nonviolent Jesus, but servants of the culture of war and empire. We want to be on Jesus' good side, but we don't want to get too close. We're used to violence, war, and empire. His talk of a kingdom of nonviolence is a dream. But for those of us brainwashed by nationalism and militarism, it seems at first like a nightmare.

What intrigues me about this Holy Week text is the word *attendant*. The word "attendant" is gentle and provocative. It speaks of someone standing nearby who waits to serve at a moment's notice, someone who attends to the other's every need, word, or request. The dictionary defines an attendant as "one who serves" or simply "being present." We think of an attendant nurse, waiting beside the patient in illness and death, or a flight attendant, whose primary task is our safety, but who also brings us a cup of coffee.

Isn't every Christian called to be an attendant of the nonviolent Jesus? In God's reign of peace, the nonviolent Jesus will have, I suppose, billions of attendants. We will all get the chance to serve and wait upon the nonviolent Jesus in his reign of universal love and infinite peace.

So Lent asks an unlikely question: Do we want to be "attendants" of the nonviolent Jesus? I suppose the honest answer is: No. We prefer to be attendants of America, its militaries and weapons and guns, its way of empire. We are used to violence; it's bred deep within us. We are brainwashed to think of violence as normal. We know how to be attendants of the president, the pope, television, the nightly news, our bank accounts, our bosses, culture, power, prestige, and ego. We know how to attend to the things of the world. But we do not know how to be attendants of Jesus.

Perhaps we think being an attendant of Jesus is encumbering. In reality, attending to America, money, war, and the culture of violence enslaves us. Attending to Jesus frees us to live in peace and love.

Lent invites us to reimagine our lives as attendants of the nonviolent Jesus. That means we need to let go of our violence and train ourselves in the way of gospel nonviolence. As attendants, we do not engage in violence or own weapons. We do not support war or empire or the U.S. military or its weapons. Instead, we choose the creative nonviolence exemplified by Jesus. We practice unconditional love, side with the poor and the enemy, show compassion, speak out for peace, and resist the culture of war and empire, come what may. And we never retaliate with further violence. As attendants of the nonviolent Jesus, we are the people who break the never-ending downward cycle of violence.

But more, we are "present" to the nonviolent Jesus as best we can. We take formal time every day to sit in silent meditation with Jesus, even if that means practicing living in the presence of Jesus. Then we try to remain with him, in his spirit, aware of him in his peace, throughout our day-to-day lives. We try to live our lives close by his side, to go through life walking with him. This is a simple, basic Christian practice. It's actually quite difficult, demanding, political, and even dangerous—yet very consoling. We're siding with a resister and a martyr, but also the God of peace. And so, the blessings are full and countless.

As we walk through Holy Week, we might practice being attendants of the nonviolent Jesus. How do we do that? Perhaps we can try first to be attendants of one another, especially those in need. We can attend to the poor, the marginalized, the sick, the elderly, the imprisoned, and the enemy. We can attend to the God of peace in our prayer. We can attend to the word of God in the gospels. We can attend to those who work for justice, disarmament, and peace. And we can attend to our own inner spirit of nonviolence so that, slowly over time, we might let go of our violence, hatreds, and resentments and cultivate interior nonviolence. Such preparations will help us become attendants of the nonviolent Jesus.

Over time, as we keep our eyes on Jesus, notice his steadfast nonviolence, begin to experiment with it, and walk out on the waters of nonviolence to meet him, we become his attendants. Soon we will desire to be in his peaceful presence at all times. If we remain faithful to him, we will find there's nowhere else we'd rather be than at his side.

QUESTIONS FOR PERSONAL REFLECTION AND JOURNALING

- *What does Jesus' description of the kingdom of God to Pilate mean for you? What does the kingdom of God as a place of nonviolence look like for you, and how can we live in that nonviolent kingdom here and now?*

- *What would it mean to live the rest of your life as an "attendant" of the nonviolent Jesus?*

- *How can we practice being "attendants" of Jesus during Lent, Holy Week, and the Easter season?*

chapter
FIFTEEN

Passers-By at Calvary

APRIL 9, 1993, WAS ONE OF MY MOST MEMORABLE GOOD
Fridays. A thousand of us gathered for a peace rally and then
marched on to the entrance of Lawrence Livermore Nuclear
Weapons Labs near San Jose, California. And there, several
hundred of us knelt in prayer—knelt in trespass, said the authorities—and submitted to arrest. It was a day to remember,
but even more so because of our guest of honor and main
speaker—Reverend William Sloane Coffin.

Coffin, the former Yale chaplain and the esteemed preacher
of New York's Riverside Church—in his day, second in preem-
inence only to Billy Graham—had agreed to teach for a semester at my theology school, the Graduate Theological Union in
Berkeley. And as organizer of the Good Friday vigil, when I
heard the news, I brashly invited him to join us.

That January, on a cold Monday afternoon, I stopped by his
spare office in Berkeley and told him enthusiastically about
our Good Friday peace plans. Would he agree to address the
crowd? He readily accepted my invitation. The vigil, he said,
would be the highlight of his semester.

A friendship soon developed, but first, he had to endure

my audacity. I, a young turk, with no experience preaching, proposed an outline for his sermon. "How about for your text," I said, "Matthew 5 and Matthew 21…?"

"Excuse me?" he asked with a smile.

I have an original idea, I announced. You could piece together these two texts and give us a great sermon. You could preach on the teaching and practice of nonviolence—the commandment to love our enemies—and Jesus' civil disobedience in the Temple. I felt sure I could show the great man a thing or two—even about preaching!

He leaned back and listened calmly, his eyes twinkling with a hint of amusement. When I finished my lengthy instruction, he said tolerantly and gently, "I was thinking more of Matthew 27:39—40: 'Those passing by reviled him, shaking their heads, and saying, "Save yourself, if you are the Son of God."'" Then he proceeded to explain his own biblical analysis of our Good Friday peace action.

"I want to say that we are no different than the passers-by at Calvary, the crowds who walked past the crucified Jesus. Thousands drive by Livermore every day. And they, too, shake their heads and say, 'Isn't it a shame? If only something could be done! If you are the Son of God, do something…' Would that be alright, John?"

"Yes, of course!" I answered with a mixture of embarrassment, wonder, and amazement.

That Good Friday morning, as the sun rose over Livermore Labs, Bill preached his powerful sermon to a stunned, enthralled crowd. He challenged us not to be passers-by, but protesters at the ongoing crucifixion of Christ among the world's poor and oppressed. And do everything you can, he said, to stop the planned nuclear crucifixion of the planet.

Many Good Fridays have come and gone since, but not

much has changed. Many of us still walk past modern-day crucifixion scenes. "If only something could be done!" we sigh. We
drive by death row, the Pentagon, Los Alamos Labs, our local
military recruiting center, and many other places of death—
and keep on driving. "If only something could be done!"

One way to look at our work for peace and justice in light of
Good Friday and Bill Coffin's acumen is to understand our true
place in the story. We do not want to be passers-by anymore.
We do not want to be soldiers or crucifiers. We do not want
to be religious or political leaders mocking those who struggle
nonviolently for justice and peace.

Instead, we want to enter the life of the crucified Jesus by
risking our own lives for justice and peace. We want to be like
Mary and John and stand with the crucified peoples of the
world.

Throughout our Good Friday world, people are once again
choosing to stand with the crucified peoples, to bear witness
for them and speak truth to power on their behalf. This week,
as I write, a handful of Pax Christi New Mexico friends held a
twenty-four-hour prayer vigil at Santa Maria de la Paz Church
in Santa Fe to mark the seventh anniversary of the U.S. crucifixion of the people of Iraq, as well as the people of Afghanistan
and Pakistan. For twenty-four hours, they read out loud the
names of the dead. Thousands of them. Dead Iraqis, Afghanis,
Pakistanis, and Americans. A litany of crucifixion.

It was an evening of sorrow, a time to face what our country has done, a time to pray for the dead and for an end to the
killing, a time to stand at the foot of the cross with the holy
women and the beloved disciple. Our vigil modeled the kind of
solidarity, spirit, and action we all need to undertake in these
Good Friday times.

"We're all Good Friday people," Buddhist leader, author, and peacemaker Joanna Macy told me recently. "And things are going to get much worse as the world collapses even more. We need to help others, to sow seeds of peace, and to teach people not to be afraid. We have to be here in the present moment with them, in this Good Friday world. But we can be on the lookout for Easter."

I hope we can continue to walk with Jesus to his Good Friday death and stand with him in the crucified peoples of the world—from Baghdad to Kabul, Camden to Detroit, Port au Prince to Congo. If we stand with him at Calvary, if we can face the world's pain and suffering with open, compassionate hearts, if we dare resist the injustice and wars that kill and hurt so many, one day we'll stand with him in the new life of resurrection peace.

QUESTIONS FOR PERSONAL
REFLECTION AND JOURNALING

- *How does the crucifixion of the nonviolent Jesus play out today in our Good Friday world? Where is Good Friday happening right now?*

- *In what ways are you a "passer-by" at the ongoing crucifixion of Christ in the world's poor and oppressed today?*

- *What do you need to do to no longer be a "passer-by," but to become someone who stands in solidarity with the crucified Christ, someone who works to stop the ongoing crucifixion of Christ in the world's poor and oppressed?*

chapter SIXTEEN

Good Friday's Last Words

ON GOOD FRIDAY, WE STAND WITH THE NONVIOLENT JESUS
as he suffers torture and execution at the hands of the empire
yet remains centered in the God of love, forgiving and nonviolent to the end. Gandhi said that in his death, Jesus practiced
perfect nonviolence. He teaches us not only how to suffer and
die but becomes a spiritual explosion of disarming love that is
still transforming us all.

On Good Friday, we listen to the words of Jesus from the
cross, as offered in the four gospels, for clues about following
him faithfully on the way of nonviolence in pursuit of justice
and peace. Here are the "seven last sayings" of the crucified,
nonviolent Jesus, for our meditation.

First, "Father, forgive them, they know not what they do" (LUKE 23:34).

Throughout his humiliation, torture, and public execution, Jesus
never yells, shows anger, threatens anyone, condemns anyone,
or says a word of violence, vengeance, or retaliation. He enters

into universal compassion for the entire human race, in perfect solidarity with everyone who suffers and dies throughout history, and so explodes into universal, nonviolent love.

Jesus reaches the heights of nonviolence by forgiving his executioners. He remains focused on the God of love, and he appeals to God to forgive us all. He says in effect, "The violence stops here in my body. You are all forgiven, but the days of killing are over."

How does he do that? I think he can do this because he focused all his energy on his compassionate, beloved God at every moment of his life. With this focus, he was also able to forgive everyone who hurt him, every day, every step along the way. Forgiveness had become his daily spiritual practice, a way of life for him, even as he trusted in his beloved God every step along the way of his tumultuous journey. Because of this daily practice, even as he was being killed, he could forgive as he had always done. Though it seems superhuman to us, it had become second nature to him. Practice makes perfect.

Forgiveness is at the heart of nonviolence. It's our entry into God's reign of peace and love. We can't enter into that realm of peace and love without forgiving everyone who has ever hurt us. We need to learn like Jesus that forgiving those who hurt us is not a one-time event but an ongoing, daily practice. We too have to forgive by name everyone who ever hurt us, every step of the way, every day. That means we are constantly forgiving. Forgiveness becomes part of our normal day-to-day life.

This is nothing new. In Mark's gospel (11:24–25), just before his arrest, Jesus tells his followers that every time they come before God in prayer, they must forgive those who hurt them. Forgiveness also stands at the center of the Lord's prayer. So it should not surprise us that the world's greatest teacher of forgiveness should practice it at the moment of his execution by the empire. Jesus always practiced first what he preached.

Good Friday is a good time to accept that we are forgiven and then to go forward and forgive ourselves and everyone who ever hurt us. If we can practice forgiveness in small everyday moments, we might be able to forgive those who hurt us in big ways. Like Jesus, we too want to go to our deaths forgiving all those who hurt us; we want to die in a spirit of compassion, peace, and universal love.

Second, "My God, my God, why have you forsaken me?" (MARK 15:34; MATTHEW 27:46; PSALM 22:1).

Jesus cries out to God, asking why God has so thoroughly rejected and abandoned him. It certainly appears that God has forsaken him. But notice: he still addresses God. Even as he dies innocently in a brutal public execution and feels that abandonment to the depth of his being, he speaks directly to God. He's still living in relationship with his beloved God. That's the key to his perfect nonviolence, his universal love, his boundless compassion. Up until his last breath, Jesus remains focused on God. That's what we have to do as well.

That may seem like a stretch, but any first-century reader of the gospel would immediately recognize this famous question as the beginning of Psalm 22, a long prayer that moves from despair, pain, and abandonment into hope, victory, and fulfillment. Indeed, by the end, it becomes a joyful celebration of resurrection.

Luke invites us into the spirit of Psalm 22, to tap into our Good Friday feelings of despair and abandonment as we work for justice and peace, and to move slowly with Jesus into new hope and possibility.

Third, "Amen, I say to you, today you will be with me in paradise" (LUKE 23:43).

Luke tells of two violent revolutionaries executed alongside Jesus. One mocks Jesus and the other defends him, saying "Jesus, remember me when you come into your kingdom." Earlier James and John asked to be at the right and left hand of Jesus, but he tells them that those places of honor are reserved by God. Now, on Good Friday, we learn who is at his right and left hand of Jesus—violent revolutionaries, executed for trying to overthrow the Roman Empire.

Does this mean Jesus sides with those in permanent resistance to empire and war, even as he remains nonviolent? Perhaps!

We need to ponder this final, shocking outcome. Jesus dies with the equivalent of El Salvador's FMLN, Nicaragua's FSLN, Northern Ireland's IRA, the P.L.O., Arab Spring rebels, and all those accused by empires of plotting revolution.

Even as he dies, Jesus ministers to the poor, the condemned, and the dying. To the one who asks, he promises a future in paradise with him. Perhaps both will join him in paradise. As followers of Jesus, we too are invited to side with those in resistance to empire, to show compassion to the poor, the condemned, and the marginalized—and of course, to work for the abolition of the death penalty.

Today in paradise? Sometimes I wonder if Luke implies that being next to Jesus, even in this Good Friday agony, near his perfect nonviolence, means that they are already in paradise, even as they die. If we too side with the condemned, the suffering, and the dying, we too are already with Christ in paradise.

The violent revolutionary who dies with Jesus at his side teaches us how to approach Jesus and how to pray. With him, our prayer now and at the hour of our death becomes, "Jesus, remember me when you come into your kingdom." Then, in peace and silence, we too await the promise.

Fourth, "Woman, behold your son. Behold your mother" (JOHN 19:26-27).

John's gospel makes it clear that women stood by the dying Jesus. The men are certainly portrayed as terrified, fearful that they too might be arrested and killed—which apparently did happen to them later on. Perhaps the men couldn't stand by the cross because they would have been immediately arrested by the authorities and crucified as his accomplices, while the women would not have been arrested. In any case, the women are faithful to Jesus and follow him even to his death and burial.

We too need to stand like the holy women, like Mary and John, with the crucified peoples of the world. Sometimes, that's all we can do—just be there, in solidarity, fully present, in shared powerlessness. That compassionate, powerless presence of loving solidarity can offer some comfort to the crucified. Indeed, it can help the peacemaker retain some sense of humanity and nonviolence.

Here in John's account, Mary and Jesus' beloved disciple, John, stand nearby. Jesus takes care of Mary by telling his beloved friend John to look after her. But I wonder if we have misread this text. Sometimes I don't think Jesus is saying, "Mother, here is your new son, my friend John, who will look after you." That may be true, but he could also be saying to his mother: "Look at me! Behold your son! This is the real me—crucified, executed, in agony, destroyed by the empire, yet nonviolent, forgiving, and compassionate to the end. I want you to really see me, to know the real me and to accept me. This is whom you are the mother of." It was a wakeup call to his mother to stop being motherly and become his disciple.

Mary knew Jesus through and through, from the womb and childhood to his death, but no one, including her, can really grasp who he is, much less understand his spectacular, loving nonviolence. Here, at the foot of the cross, Jesus tells her to "behold your son." Mary may have been the only one to ever really see Jesus.

Like Mary, we need to do the same—to behold the crucified, nonviolent Jesus: to really look at him, see him as he is, accept him in all his scandalous, dangerous, holy, glorious nonviolence, and fashion our lives after his nonviolent spirit so that we too might become mature disciples.

Fifth, "I thirst" (JOHN 19:28).

Throughout the Gospel of John, Jesus is thirsty. When he meets the Samaritan woman at the well of Jacob, he asks her for a drink of water. They get talking, he confides in her that he is the messiah, and she runs off and tells the whole town about him.

But he never gets a drink! Later, in the temple, he cries out, "Let anyone who thirsts come to me and drink!" (John 7:37). In Matthew, he says, "I was thirsty and you gave me drink." Here in John, they offer him wine, and he takes it. In other accounts, he refuses the wine, saying he will not drink again until he drinks "the new wine at table in my Father's kingdom." By refusing the wine, he feels every pulse of pain. He goes to his death fully conscious of every pulse of pain.

This line was one of the most important Scripture verses for Mother Teresa. She reflected on its meaning for decades and developed her own spirituality about the God who thirsts for humanity's love and never receives it. Good Friday invites us to hear the thirst of Jesus and to try to quench that thirst in our prayer and loving service of others. We want to be the people who give the nonviolent Jesus a cup of water, who quench his thirst, who love him as he is, and serve him in his poor, thirsty, crucified people.

Sixth, *"It is finished"* (JOHN 19:30).

The hour has finally arrived—the journey complete, the work done, the mission accomplished. "And bowing his head, he handed over his spirit." Jesus was determined to fulfill his mission as the beloved Son of God, the peacemaking Christ. Does it seem like he "successfully" finished his mission? Wasn't he a total failure? Or did he indeed finish his mission perfectly, as far as the God of peace, love, and compassion is concerned?

"It is finished," he says as he dies, in John's account. This sentence invites us to give thanks for Jesus and his mission and to reflect on how we intend to finish our own missions. How can we join Jesus' mission and spend the rest of our lives fulfilling his work of peace, love, and nonviolence so that we too can say at our deaths, in a spirit of grace and gratitude, "It is finished. I have fulfilled my mission. I have faithfully followed the nonviolent Jesus and done my small part to bring peace and love to humanity"?

Good Friday invites us to reflect on the mission before us and how we intend to see it to completion as faithful followers of the nonviolent Jesus.

Seventh, *"Father, into your hands I commend my spirit"* (LUKE 23:46).

Jesus offers himself completely to his beloved God, who announced to him by the Jordan River, "You are my beloved." Jesus lives and dies in intimate relationship with his beloved God. That is the key to his peacemaking life and death—he is faithful to his core identity and his relationship to his beloved

God. With his last breath, in Luke's version, he surrenders himself unconditionally to his beloved God. "Father, into your hands I commend my spirit."

This last sentence summons us to be faithful to our true identities as sons and daughters of the God of peace and to that same intimate relationship with God and one another.

In the Sermon on the Mount, Jesus calls his people of gospel nonviolence "the sons and daughters of God." "Blessed are the peacemakers, they are the sons and daughters of the God of peace." "Love your enemies, then you will be sons and daughters of the God who lets the sun shine on the good and the bad and the rain fall on the just and the unjust." The gospel invites us to claim our true identities as sons and daughters of the God of peace and love and to remain faithful to them as peacemakers and people of universal love. From the desert to the cross, Jesus resisted the temptation to deny his true identity, to doubt God. He trusted in the God of peace and, in the end, surrendered to God. Because of this fidelity, he remained perfectly nonviolent. He wants us to do the same.

His holy death invites us to refocus ourselves on our beloved God, to be faithful to our true identities, and to surrender ourselves to God. As we ponder, pray over, and prepare for our own deaths, we may want to take these words as our own and to cultivate that interior attitude of unconditional surrender to God. If we want to be able to say them on the day of our own deaths, we need to start saying them now; we need to live our way into that loving surrender of peace.

The Loud Cry

But there's more. According to Mark, as Jesus dies of suffocation, he uses his last ounce of strength to gather all his energy and give one last outburst, "a loud cry." With that, he breathes his last breath. He has no more strength to lift his lungs and take another breath. He dies fully conscious, alert, and alive. In Mark 15:34–37, we read:

> At three o'clock, Jesus cried out in a loud voice, "My God, my God, why have you forsaken me?" Some of the bystanders who heard it said, "Look, he is calling Elijah." One of them ran, soaked a sponge with wine, put it on a reed, and gave it to him to drink, saying, "Wait, let us see if Elijah comes to take him down." Jesus gave a loud cry and breathed his last.

Jesus has always lived a life of total nonviolent resistance. He has done everything he can to awaken people to reality. I think he decided to use the moment of his death as one last gift. He offers his last dying breath as one last act of protest against the world of killing, war, and empire. He gathers his last ounce of strength, takes one last deep breath, and, instead of dying quietly, he bursts out with a loud cry. After all his teachings, parables, commandments, beatitudes, and blessings, he cries out loudly in an appeal beyond silence and words. He cries out to God and to every human heart. It is his last act.

This Good Friday, I invite us to hear the loud cry of the crucified, nonviolent Jesus. Where do we hear it? I hear it in the cry of the poor and oppressed throughout history and throughout the world today; in all the victims of war, injustice, and empire; in the victims of Hiroshima and Nagasaki, Auschwitz and Dresden, Vietnam and Central America, Iraq and Afghanistan, Libya and Syria, Congo and Palestine. In that loud cry, I hear Jesus begging humanity to wake up, reject the insanity of violence, become nonviolent, turn with compassion toward others, and welcome God's reign of peace.

This Good Friday, as we hear his last words and his loud cry, we let our hearts be broken and disarmed, and we surrender to the God of peace all over again.

QUESTIONS FOR PERSONAL REFLECTION AND JOURNALING

- *As we pray over Good Friday and the last words of Jesus, how can we learn to forgive everyone as Jesus did? How can we move from despair to hope, as in Psalm 22? Do we want to be with Jesus in paradise? How can we behold the crucified Jesus? Where do we see him today? How can we relieve the thirst of Jesus? How can we live the rest of our lives so that we might fulfill our mission? How do we surrender ourselves to God?*

- *Where do we hear the "loud cry" of the crucified Christ today? How do we respond?*

- *How does Jesus practice nonviolence throughout his suffering right up to his death, and how can we better practice nonviolence in our lives?*

chapter SEVENTEEN

THE CROSS AS THE WAY

THROUGHOUT HISTORY, CHRISTIANS HAVE SPOKEN OF "the way of the cross" or "taking up our cross" or "carrying our cross." These days, however, few people speak about walking the way of the cross. The cross is old fashioned, out of date, irrelevant to our modern sensibilities. It doesn't fit into our world of entertainment and creature comforts.

At one point not long ago, we might have lamented, "Oh, I've got a flat tire; I'm carrying my cross," or "I've got a difficult in-law, and it's my cross," or "I have a tough boss, and it's just the cross I have to bear."

But for the nonviolent Jesus and the writers of the four gospels, the cross was the natural consequence of revolutionary nonviolence, civil disobedience, and prophetic truth-telling. Sooner or later, the ruling authorities were going to arrest him, torture him, and execute him, as they always do with trouble-making revolutionaries.

In Jesus' day, the cross was a total scandal. It was capital punishment by the empire for capital crime, for resisting the empire.

For the nonviolent Jesus, then, the way of the cross is active nonviolent resistance to systemic injustice, to empire, to the culture of war. In a world of total war, it defines the public work of making peace, loving others, struggling for justice and disarmament, and serving God. It's the way to salvation, the way to welcome God's reign of peace and nonviolence here on earth. It's the Christian phrase that sums up the practice of gospel nonviolence in a world of violence.

A few thoughts, then, about the cross.

Martin Luther King Jr. taught that "unearned suffering love is always redemptive." He taught the dynamic of the cross through the practice of creative nonviolence—in his case, against the systemic racism of segregation. If we dare resist segregation through the methodology of nonviolence, insist on the truth of our equality but do so through nonviolent love, and accept the consequences of harassment or jail without vengeance or retaliation, eventually the scales will fall from the eyes of our opponents, they will recognize the error of their ways and the truth of equality, and a new day of freedom will be born. The cross was a methodology of social, political transformation, but it was risky, as the deaths of several civil rights activists showed.

In other words, the cross is not just a symbol or a metaphor but a methodology, a particular way of organizing and living—in this case, in peaceful resistance to the culture of war and injustice. As people who carry the cross, we resist all the forces of death, war, and injustice and do so with every weapon of nonviolence at our disposal. Gandhi, Dr. King, and all the leaders and nonviolent movements for positive social change in modern history advocate the methodology of the cross as a way to transform society into a more just, peaceful realm.

The way of the cross, then, is also the way of the nonviolent martyrs of justice and peace, including Gandhi and Dr. King, as well as Franz Jagerstatter, Oscar Romero, Ita Ford, Maura Clarke, Dorothy Kazel, Jean Donovan, Dorothy Stang, and Steve Biko. These heroes who paid the ultimate price of their lives on behalf of humanity followed the nonviolent Jesus on the way of the cross all the way unto their own deaths at the hands of the state. In turn, their nonviolent suffering love touched the hearts of millions and transformed society for the better.

As followers of the nonviolent Jesus who walk in his footsteps, we walk the way of the cross, doing our part to support the nonviolent movements for justice and peace, in resistance to the culture of war and injustice. We pray for the grace to give our lives for suffering humanity, for the coming of God's reign of nonviolence here on earth. In doing so, we live consciously, mindfully, fully alive and alert, trying to be as nonviolent as Jesus every step of the way, even toward our own deaths.

In going to his death with such deliberate, mindful nonviolence, Jesus teaches us how to live and how to die. He shows us how to go to our own deaths—not in fear, not with anxiety, not in despair, not in doubt, not in hatred, but in the light, grace, and peace of our own loving nonviolence.

As people of the cross, we stay centered, prayerful, and mindful, trusting in the God of peace, keeping our eyes on the risen Jesus, letting go of ourselves, accepting our powerlessness, and surrendering our very being to the God of peace. We give our lives for suffering humanity, doing our best to support God's work to disarm the world and to go to our own deaths in faith, hope, and love, knowing that we have done our part by living nonviolent lives and supporting the global grassroots movements of nonviolence. Along the way, we catch a glimpse of resurrection and taste its peace. As we befriend our deaths and go to God in peace, our lives and even our deaths become a gift to others and bear the good fruit of peace.

QUESTIONS FOR PERSONAL
REFLECTION AND JOURNALING

- *What does it mean to carry the cross or walk the way of the cross? How do you accompany Jesus as he carries his cross in the world today?*

- *As Dr. King explained, how is the cross a methodology for social change?*

- *Do you agree with Dr. King that "unearned suffering love is always redemptive"?*

- *How can we befriend our deaths so that they bear the good fruit of peace?*

chapter EIGHTEEN

There On the Shore Stood Jesus, and It Was Morning

AFTER THE BETRAYAL, ARREST, TRIAL, TORTURE, AND execution of Jesus, the story that follows is so utterly fantastic that it, if true, changes the very nature of reality. Turns out, death does not get the last word. Jesus rises and lives on and even maintains his spectacular peace and nonviolence. A cosmic shift has occurred. The door of resurrection has been opened. Eternal life has begun now. Everything Jesus said and taught and did has been verified and affirmed as true. Therefore, he's the one person worth listening to. That is, if the story is true.

And there's the rub. We either choose to believe in resurrection or not. Speaking for myself, I choose to believe in resurrection and the risen Jesus. The story and the teachings make most sense in light of his resurrection. And because I choose to believe in resurrection, the risen Jesus, and his resurrection gift of peace, I try to practice and walk his way of nonviolence.

I love that beautiful sentence from John 21, describing one of those first Easter encounters. It's a kind of Zen scene in perfect mindfulness that opens up new peace and life within us: "There on the shore stood Jesus, and it was morning."

He's alive, healed, smiling, gracious, and peaceful, standing there on the shore as the sun rises over the beautiful Sea of Galilee. He's still gentle, loving, forgiving, and nonviolent. He hasn't changed. He's not a triumphant judge, come to condemn the disciples or the rest of us. There's not a trace of anger, resentment, retaliation, or vengeance. There's no argument, no "I told you so," no condemnation. Instead, he makes breakfast for the disciples. "Come have breakfast," he says with a smile.

We move from the Last Supper to the First Breakfast!

If any of us had been through such a horrific ordeal—betrayal, arrest, denial, torture, execution, and resurrection—would our first task be to make breakfast for the friends who had abandoned us? Most of us would probably not even come back.

His friends are out at sea, exhausted from working all night and catching nothing. They hear someone call out, suggesting they throw their nets in the other direction. They make a huge catch, recognize him, and rush to the shore, overcome, overwhelmed, astounded, speechless. He serves them breakfast, and they sit around his charcoal fire in silence, looking at him, saying nothing, enjoying the new day.

A perfect Zen moment, the present moment of peace, the Eschaton, with Jesus fully alive and the disciples coming to life. In contrast to the violence of the world—from Hiroshima to Vietnam to Iraq, from the Pentagon to Livermore Labs to Los Alamos—here we have a scene of quintessential peace—"peace on earth," the God of peace at peace with his friends, enjoying a picnic by the shore. Here finally is no violence, no fear, no resentment, no retaliation, no guns, no killing, no war, no empire, no death. Here we get a taste of the peace and new life in Jesus' kingdom of nonviolence.

But as usual, the gospel doesn't leave it there. The nonviolent Jesus shortly gets down to business. His friend Simon Peter had only days before denied three times knowing Jesus. Simon Peter had warmed his hands over the "charcoal" fire in the imperial Roman courtyard while Jesus was tried and tortured inside. Yet now, we are told, Jesus has built his own "charcoal" fire (the only two times that word "charcoal" is used in the Bible). Simon Peter now warms himself and enjoys breakfast in the courtyard of peace, the courtyard of the nonviolent Jesus. The setting is warm, friendly, intimate, and comes with an invitation.

In contrast to the imperial courtyard where Simon Peter denied knowing Jesus three times, Simon Peter is given three opportunities to redeem himself in the courtyard of peace. If it were us, we might get mad at Simon Peter, express our hurt and bewilderment, demand to know why, and beg for Simon Peter's apology. But the risen Jesus, nonviolent as usual, goes right to the heart of the matter. "Do you love me?" he asks Simon Peter.

In 1985, I heard Henri Nouwen give a one-and-a-half-hour sermon on this text. This is the most important question of the Bible, Henri insisted. God asks each one of us: "Do you love me? Do you love me? Do you truly love me?" This question requires weeks, months, and years of reflection. As Rilke suggested, it's best to live with the questions so we might live our way into the answers.

Here Jesus reveals his need for friendship, love, and commitment. He vulnerably opens his heart. But in the original Greek, we notice that Jesus invites Simon Peter not just to profess love, but *"agape,"* "unconditional, sacrificial, nonviolent love." The question is: "Do you *agape* me?" Alas, Simon Peter's answer, we also note in the Greek, falls short. "Yes, I *philia* you, Jesus," he says. "*Philia*" is the Greek word for "limited love," the love for relatives, friends, and neighbors, as opposed to *agape*, the "unlimited," universal love of Christ.

Simon Peter doesn't quite get it, so Jesus asks him again, and again. Alas, Simon Peter never offers *agape*. He can only promise the limited love of *philia*. After each response, Jesus gives him a mission. "Feed my lambs. Tend my sheep. Feed my sheep." If you love me, he says, then serve my people.

This exchange invites us to consider the kind of love we hold for the nonviolent Jesus, and thus for sisters and brothers around the world. Do we go only as far as Simon Peter, with the limited love of *philia*, or can we practice the unlimited love for Jesus and show the same unconditional love he has for us, the love of *agape*?

At the end of the story, for the first time in John's gospel, after everything Simon Peter has been through—all the journeys, healings, confrontations, and civil disobedience, after the arrest, execution, and resurrection of Jesus—now, in this place, Simon Peter is called, for the first time, to discipleship.

The journey, he learns, is only just beginning!

"When you were younger, you dressed yourself and did what you please. Now someone will put a belt around you and lead you where you would rather not go. Follow me" (21:18–19).

Dear Simon Peter, Jesus says, if you really love me, follow me on the road to peace. Now it's your turn to walk to Jerusalem, to Rome, or to Washington, DC, to resist empire and announce God's reign of peace. Practice my way, truth, and life of loving nonviolence. Take a stand against war, poverty, nuclear weapons, and the culture of death. You too may have to suffer and give your life, but take heart—death does not get the last word.

You too will rise and live in my reign of peace forever.

Simon Peter must have been surprised and shocked. So are we. Too often we think that we've done everything we could. We lived a good life, gave it a good try. We said our prayers, did good deeds, tried to take a stand. We've watched presidents come and go, wars heat up and end, weapons be built and used, corruption reach unimaginable heights, even the weather threatened by our greed. We're older and ready to slow down. We deserve to sit back and take it easy. And deep down, we still nurture our fear. Our own love, alas, is quite limited. We have yet to break free into *agape*, the unconditional, universal, nonviolent love of Jesus.

Just at this moment, when we think we've seen it all, we're called to follow the nonviolent Jesus, like Simon Peter, all over again, as if for the first time.

Easter is the time to begin again, to take up the journey of peace and nonviolence in the footsteps of the risen Jesus all over again. The gospel suggests that if we truly love Jesus, then we will do whatever he asks, even live as he lived, give as he gave, love as he loved, serve as he served, disarm as he disarmed, resist empire as he resisted empire, and die with compassion and forgiveness as he did. Like Simon Peter, we start all over and follow him—even to where we would rather not go. We can do this because we see the nonviolent Jesus alive and well, we know his way of nonviolence has been vindicated, and we know that as his friends our survival is guaranteed.

The fifty days of Easter are a good time to taste the new life of resurrection peace, to center ourselves in resurrection peace, and to begin again the journey of discipleship in resurrection peace. We imagine the risen Jesus standing at dawn on the shore. We share that intimate breakfast with him, see his wounds, receive his gift of peace, tell him we love him, and hear his call to follow. These beautiful Easter days can resurrect the spirit of hope, love, life, and nonviolence within us, so that, like Simon Peter, we too can be transformed into people of universal nonviolent love for Christ in humanity and share that resurrection peace with the world of war, poverty, and empire.

If Jesus is not risen, St. Paul says, we are fools. But if he is risen, then God has affirmed his nonviolence, called us to practice his nonviolence, guaranteed our survival, and summoned us to give our lives in *agape* love for justice and peace.

"I shall die, but that is all I shall do for death," the poet Edna St. Vincent Millay wrote. From now on, we have nothing to do with death and the culture of death. We resist death, live life to the full, and go forward in hope with Jesus' gift of peace for one and all.

Easter invites us to spend our lives breathing in the spirit of resurrection peace, becoming people of resurrection nonviolence, sharing resurrection *agape*, manifesting resurrection forgiveness, speaking resurrection peace to the world, and embarking anew on the path of life with the risen Jesus.

With the resurrection of the nonviolent Jesus, filled with new hope and vitality, we learn a new vocabulary, the language of peace and nonviolence, beginning with an ancient Christian word: "Alleluia!"

QUESTIONS FOR PERSONAL
REFLECTION AND JOURNALING

- *How does Jesus continue to manifest peace and nonviolence in the resurrection accounts? What does it mean for us that he shows no anger, no resentment, no bitterness, and no spirit of revenge?*

  ....

- *How do we accept Jesus' resurrection gift of peace?*

  ....

- *How do we answer Jesus' question, "Do you love (agape) me?" How can we fulfill his mission to feed his lambs, and tend and feed his sheep? How are we, like Simon Peter, being called to follow Jesus all over again, even to go where we would rather not go?*

  ....

- *What does resurrection mean for us?*

chapter
NINETEEN

"What Things?"

THERE THEY ARE, TWO CRESTFALLEN DISCIPLES, WALKING down the road after Jesus' horrific torture and execution. Fearful and grief-stricken, they're clearing out of Jerusalem and drifting toward Emmaus. In other words, they're walking away, walking the wrong way, leaving everything behind.

But then their story takes a turn. Someone sidles up to the two. We're told it's Jesus—even though he was just executed. So he's risen from the dead, alive and well. But his friends do not recognize him.

"What are you discussing as you walk along?" he asks them. They stop and turn. "Are you the only person in Jerusalem who does not know the things that have happened in these last days?"

The risen Jesus then asks one of the most astonishing questions in the entire Bible: "What things?" (Luke 24:19).

Now, had it been us—had we performed miracles, healed the sick, and held aloft the banner of nonviolence, only to be betrayed, abandoned, executed, and raised—we would invariably have launched into a breathless account. "You wouldn't believe what I've been through! I was killed. Then I was raised.

Now I'm back!" We might launch into an attack on our friends too, asking, "How could you leave me? Why did you doubt me? Why didn't you accompany me all the way?"

The humble, nonviolent Jesus instead draws out his friends. "What things?"

I suppose Jesus wants us to tell him his story in our own lives. He wants to hear our experience of God. He wants us to share our journeys with him so he can show us how he is right there beside us. This, he knows, is how hope is reborn.

Luke 24 keeps reticent about the details. But the reader surmises the gist of the wayfarers' talk: Jesus' apparent defeat, the agony of the execution, their dashed hopes, and the plain fact that they do not see him anymore. And then on the air was a wild tale of an empty tomb. What to make of that?

They get the stranger up to date, and toward the end their very grammar sums up their despondency. In the original Greek, a specific verb tense comes into play, the past pluperfect: "We had hoped..."

We had hoped!

"We had hoped things would change. We had hoped war, empire, and occupations would cease. We had hoped God would intervene. We had hoped justice would come. We had hoped humanity would live in peace and care for its poor and protest in favor of all creatures and creation. We had hoped death would not get the last word. We had hoped Jesus would lead us to peace."

Once we had hope. Now we have none.

Try this mental exercise. Enter the scene; place yourself as one of the downcast disciples. Likely you will find their despair resonating in your own heart. Like me, you'll recall the many past pluperfects that have sounded from your own lips. "God, are you the only One who doesn't see what's happening?

Nonviolence hasn't made much of a difference. Corporations still squander, wars still rage in our name, the American empire crushes the world's poor, nuclear weapons still hang on hair-trigger alert, catastrophic climate change bears down on all of us like a global tornado. We had hoped. We had hoped Jesus' reign of peace would break through here and now."

But now imagine this. The stranger tells us, "How foolish you are! How slow you are to believe all that the prophets spoke! Was it not necessary that the Messiah should suffer these things and enter into his glory?"

Our despair persists. "Necessary? What difference did it make? The world brims still with injustice, starvation, and war. We stand on the brink of total environmental destruction. Nuclear weapons are stockpiled, and billions of people are in poverty."

And: "Your nonviolent way has been thoroughly rejected. Greed and violence rule the world. And the church falls into line. Afraid to die, in love with the culture of death, it keeps nonviolence at arm's length. Seems things are worse now than during your days on earth."

But Jesus will not cooperate with our despair. He embodies hope. He was crucified but is now raised from the dead, and he starts afresh with the two disciples—and also with us.

He explains again the story of salvation. He outlines the Scriptures. He reviews the journey of faith from Moses through the prophets and the psalms to himself. He tutors them again on the biblical path of nonviolent resistance—the very path that leads to the cross. And then to new life and glory. He invites the two of them—and the rest of us—to understand the wisdom of the paschal mystery.

The Christ has not failed his mission, he explains. Death and empire have fallen. The culture of destruction is crumbling. The old world is falling away. Triumphant is the way of nonviolence. Christ has been raised. The God of love and peace is glorified. The new realm of God's peace and justice is at hand. Even creation will be renewed. Suffering accepted in love in the pursuit of truth and justice bears immeasurable fruit, if one only believes and holds out for the long haul. As Dr. King would later say: truth crushed to earth will rise again.

And this: notice how the way of peace, the grassroots of gospel nonviolence, lives on through history to disarm the world, from Jonah and Isaiah to Francis and Claire to Gandhi and Dorothy Day, from the abolitionists and the suffragists to the civil rights movement and the anti-apartheid movement, from the feminist movement to the gay and lesbian movement, from the fall of the Berlin Wall to the Arab Spring—a new world has begun.

The stranger has the two travelers mesmerized. They urge him to stay and eat. There, at the table, he takes the bread, blesses it, breaks it, and shares it—and they recognize him. Jesus—in the form of a stranger, a refugee, an immigrant, an outcast, a homeless person—is now revealed in their midst as the risen God of peace. And their hearts burn within them. They are on fire. In their sharing with him, there is born in them a new hope for peace, a hope Jesus ratifies.

That evening, he appears to his community with the ineffable greeting, "Peace be with you. Repentance, forgiveness, and peace will be preached now to all the nations, beginning from Jerusalem. You are witnesses to these things."

Here, to my mind, is the story of all stories. It bears us along from despair to new hope. It urges us, through the risen Jesus, to cling to hope. It calls us to join the peace and justice movements of salvation history. It summons us to enter the stream of resurrection flowing through time. It draws us to spend our lives in the nonviolent struggle for life. It pushes us into the outlandish hope of the nonviolent risen Jesus. From now on, we too will be his witnesses, disciples, apostles, and prophets of peace, love, and nonviolence.

That new fire turns us around—literally. We set off but this time reverse our tracks. We forsake the road to Emmaus, the journey of despair, and return to Jerusalem, the scene of the crime. There, hope and faith undermine empire. And in fearless nonviolent action, we take up the work of the risen Christ. He lives on in us. The story continues because we start walking the way all over again.

During the Easter season, I invite us to look beyond the headlines and top stories of the culture of despair, a culture on the road to Emmaus. Let's ask ourselves: How can we move beyond the past pluperfect? What gives us new hope? What makes our hearts blaze? What makes us turn around? Where do we encounter the risen Jesus? What inspires us to join the work of resurrection? How can we rise up with new energy to face the culture of violence and war, and carry on Jesus' campaign of nonviolence?

In other words, how can we be witnesses to "these things"?

QUESTIONS FOR PERSONAL
REFLECTION AND JOURNALING

- *Where do we meet the risen Jesus today? Where do we see him in history, especially the history of justice and peace movements?*

   ....

- *What does the risen Jesus ask us? How do we tell Jesus his ongoing story in our own lives?*

   ....

- *What gives us hope today? What makes us burn within and energizes us to carry on the gospel work for justice and peace?*

   ....

- *How can we be witnesses of these things, of the resurrection, of the nonviolent Jesus?*

chapter
TWENTY

THE RESURRECTION GIFT OF PEACE, THE NEW LIFE OF NONVIOLENCE

A FEW YEARS AGO, I SERVED AS THE PASTOR OF THE LITTLE mission church of San Jose de Picacho along the U.S.-Mexico border. I remember one Holy Week vividly. It was hot, nearly 90 degrees, with wind gusts over 50 mph. I took time to walk along the drought-afflicted Rio Grande and found myself on retreat, with time to consider the events of Holy Thursday, Good Friday, and Easter Sunday.

"This is Eisenhower's military-industrial complex," one parishioner told me. The whole region is militarized by our troops on one side, and Juarez, Mexico, on the other side, where tens of thousands have been killed in drug wars in recent years. They send us drugs; we send them guns. They cross the border to get away from poverty; we spend billions to keep them away, to send them back, or to arrest and imprison them.

128

"Love your neighbor" is not the standard down here. A few miles away stands Fort Bliss, the U.S. Army's second-largest base. Next door is White Sands Missile Range, the largest army base, where every type of missile, rocket, and bomb has been first tested and exploded, including the first nuclear weapon at the nearby "Trinity Site" beyond the nuclear town of Alamagordo.

During our Good Friday evening service, someone dumped a body along a desert road less than a mile away. This is not a land of resurrection, I realized, but a place of crucifixion and death.

At the Easter Vigil and Easter Sunday Mass, I asked the congregation to think what resurrection means for them. Do we rejoice that Jesus has been raised from the dead? Are we glad that he's alive and well? If so, what then? Do we go about our day-to-day lives unchanged "even if someone should rise from the dead"? What does his resurrection have to do with our gun violence, bombing raids, executions, drone attacks, nuclear weapons, global poverty, and environmental destruction? If it makes no difference in our lives and our violent world, then we might as well go Easter egg hunting on the White House lawn or just give up on hope and life.

Walking along the desert border land and the Rio Grande, I found myself thinking about the politics of resurrection. We barely know what nonviolent politics might look like. Most of us, from Bush to Obama, to our relatives, to our local priests and bishops, uphold the politics of crucifixion. We support our military, justify our war-making, advocate revenge, pay for our drones, even support executions. We honor those involved in the mass murder of war. Indeed, we kill people who kill people to show that killing people is wrong.

We are experts at the politics of crucifixion. We are told that our wars are necessary, our weapons defensive, our nuclear power plants safe, our tax breaks for billionaires a sign of freedom, and climate change a lie. The mainstream media hardly ever points to another way. No alternative voices are permitted to speak. (And so, boycott the *New York Times* and the *Washington Post,* as well as the network news, FOX, CNN, and all spokespeople for the culture of war and death.)

The U.S. killing of Osama bin Laden epitomized for me our politics of crucifixion. What came from that public execution? Didn't it just add to the cycle of death, justify our mad violence, and ensure future terrorist attacks against us? If we believe in democracy, didn't he deserve a fair trial before a jury? As my friend Scott Wright wrote, the death of this one man came at the price of "ten years of war—with no end in sight; hundreds of thousands of lives lost—including 6,000 U.S. soldiers; trillions of dollars wasted—and a military budget that has doubled from $350 billion to $700 billion; torture of prisoners and no accountability for those who torture. The global war on terror, which sought to end terror, has instead made war and terror a permanent fixture of our fragile planet."

But what about the politics of resurrection? As resurrection people, I told my parishioners on the border, we have nothing to do with death. We do not support the forces of death. We do not bring death to anyone. We get rid of our guns, resist militarism, seek to dismantle weapons, and try to transform our culture of death. We are people of nonviolence, forgiveness, compassion, and peace. We see the coming of Christ's reign of life and resurrection, where there is no more death, no more war, no more violence, no more tears.

The resurrection accounts that we read in the Easter season offer clues about this new life of nonviolence. When the risen Jesus appears to the disciples, he says, "Peace be with you."

They welcome his peace and rejoice in his presence. Despite the insanity of the nation and the world, as resurrection people, we, too, try to welcome that peace in our hearts and our personal lives, to become people of personal peace.

Then he breathes on them and gives them the Holy Spirit. So we breathe in the Holy Spirit and "conspire" with Jesus in this new life of love, nonviolence, and peace. He commends forgiveness and community, and then says, "You are my witnesses. Go and make disciples of all the nations." So we take up the challenge. We pledge to be his witnesses of peace, to go forth as his apostles of nonviolence, to invite everyone into discipleship to this new way of resurrection peace and nonviolence.

The political implications of resurrection offer not just hope—but our only hope. If we believe in resurrection and look toward Christ's reign of nonviolence, then we are summoned into a new vocation of peacemaking. We have to reject revenge, retaliation, guns, killing, and war, and join the global grassroots campaigns to abolish war, poverty, executions, nuclear weapons, and environmental destruction.

While the U.S. government carries on the tired old politics of crucifixion, there are breakthroughs happening every day that herald the radical hope of resurrection. We rarely see them in the mainstream media, but they exist in the movements of nonviolent resistance sweeping through the Middle East, where people are awakening from decades of fear and giving their lives to resist oppressive regimes—in Egypt, Tunisia, Yemen, Syria, Bahrain, and Palestine. These movements are also growing in Africa and Latin America and around the world. We see them in the four hundred thousand people who marched against environmental destruction in New York City on September 21, 2014, and the thousands who marched against war, poverty, and environmental destruction in over two hundred nonviolent actions in every state that following week, under the banner of "Campaign Nonviolence." (See *www.campaignnonviolence.org.*)

That awakening needs to spread. We need a nonviolent revolution here at home that will push for the dismantling of our nuclear arsenal and our empire, reverse our senseless military spending, end our global domination, protect creation, and guarantee housing, food, education, employment, and health care for all. Then, as we educate one another in the ways of nonviolent conflict resolution, the healing of humanity can begin.

The resurrection of Jesus was ignored by the culture of war and death in his day, but it was an earthquake in reality. It marked the beginning of the end of the Roman Empire and the beginning of a grassroots, community-based movement of loving nonviolence that continues to transform humanity. Our small efforts for peace seem to be ignored by the culture of war and death, but if we continue to build that grassroots movement, the pressure builds for a seismic shift in the political plates that undergird our war-making world. We have to go forward in that faith, in that resurrection spirit.

As more and more of us begin to understand the nonviolence of Jesus and create more peaceful lives, we too let go of our fear, anger, and despair. By withdrawing our cooperation in the big business of money and war, we take the steam out of the war machine and welcome God's reign of peace. By joining the grassroots movements of nonviolence for the disarmament of the world and justice for the world's poor, we become witnesses of the resurrection. We carry on the work of the risen, nonviolent Jesus.

With his resurrection, we take heart once more, trust him completely, and go forward in faith, hope, and love, walking the Way.

QUESTIONS FOR PERSONAL REFLECTION AND JOURNALING

- *How do we see the imperial politics of crucifixion play out in the world today? What are the political implications of the resurrection of the nonviolent Jesus? What does his resurrection mean in our own lives?*

- *How do we go forth and make nonviolent disciples of all nations? How can we teach and preach and spread the way of nonviolence far and wide?*

- *What grassroots movement of nonviolence for justice and disarmament are you part of, or can you join? How are you part of the risen Jesus' ongoing movement for justice, disarmament, and peace?*

CONCLUSION

As we follow in the footsteps of the nonviolent Jesus, we become walkers of the Way. Every day, we walk the way of peace, mindfulness, nonviolence, compassion, and love. We take life one step at a time. We live every moment in the present moment of peace. We breathe in the fullness of life and love and offer life and love wherever we go. We join the global grassroots movements of nonviolence for the coming of a new world without war, poverty, nuclear weapons, and environmental destruction. We walk through the world like the nonviolent Jesus and, in the process, carry on Jesus' work of peace, justice, love, and nonviolence.

Along the way, we unpack the social, economic, and political implications of gospel peace and nonviolence. We are not afraid, in our universal love, to speak out against killing, war, injustice, and weapons. We are not afraid to rock the boat of the unjust status quo. We are not afraid to take public nonviolent action for justice for the poor, for disarmament, for the protection of creation and its creatures. We are not afraid of death, and so we walk forward into the world of violence and war with the good news of peace, love, and nonviolence as followers of the risen, nonviolent Jesus. We announce the coming of God's reign of peace and nonviolence here and now.

As walkers of the Way, we become agents of nonviolent social change in our communities and nation. We become instruments of God's peace and join the lineage of saints from Francis of Assisi to Dorothy Day of New York. We sow seeds of peace that one day in the future will give forth a new harvest of peace with justice.

Lent is a good time to take stock of our lives, to return again to the nonviolent Jesus, and to see where we are on the Way. Are we still walking in the footsteps of Jesus, or did we get stuck along the way? Do we teach and model nonviolence for others, or does violence still linger within us, the culture of war still hold sway over us? Do we want to go deeper still into the peace, love, and nonviolence of Jesus, or are we burnt out, cynical, and hopeless? Where are we on the road to peace?

Lent offers a holy time to reflect on Jesus' spectacular journey of nonviolence from Galilee to Jerusalem, where he confronted systemic injustice, instituted a new covenant of nonviolence, ordered his followers to put down the sword, underwent arrest, torture, and execution in a spirit of steadfast nonviolence, and rose to give us his peace and a new mission to carry on his Way.

During Lent, we realize once again that the nonviolent Jesus does not teach us how to kill, how to bomb, how to execute, how to nuke our enemies, how to make money, how to be successful, or how to dominate others. We discover anew that the nonviolent Jesus teaches us how to live, how to love, how to pray, how to serve, how to worship, how to heal, how to act, how to be nonviolent, how to resist injustice, how to make peace, how to forgive, how to suffer, and how to die.

As his followers, we renew our discipleship once again. We decide to take him at his word, unlearn the lessons of violence we have been taught, retrain ourselves in his way of loving nonviolence, and determine to carry on his mission as best we can.

As walkers of the Way, we take personally the mission he gave to his first followers, after his resurrection. "As the Father sent me, so I send you," he told them after wishing them peace. Today, he wants to send each one of us on that mission of peace. He missions us to go forth as gospel peacemakers into the culture of violence and war.

And so, we get up and get going. We walk on and follow the Way. We may not know where the path leads, nor do we know what exactly lies ahead, but we are walkers of the Way, and there's a new spring in our step. Up ahead, we see light on the horizon. We know for sure now—God's reign of peace is at hand. The time has come to tell the world all over again.

So we take another step forward.

ABOUT THE AUTHOR

John Dear has spent over three decades speaking to people around the world about the gospel of Jesus, the way of nonviolence, and the call to make peace. He has served as the director of the Fellowship of Reconciliation, the largest interfaith peace organization in the United States, and after September 11, 2001, as one of the Red Cross coordinators of chaplains at the Family Assistance Center, and counseled thousands of relatives and rescue workers. He has worked in homeless shelters, soup kitchens, and community centers; traveled in war zones around the world, including Iraq, Palestine, Nicaragua, Afghanistan, and Colombia; lived in El Salvador, Guatemala, and Northern Ireland; been arrested over seventy-five times in acts of civil disobedience against war; and spent eight months in prison for a Plowshares disarmament action. In the 1990s, he arranged for Mother Teresa to speak to various governors to stop the death penalty. He has two master's degrees in Theology from the Graduate Theological Union in California, and has taught theology at Fordham University. Recently, Archbishop Desmond Tutu and several others nominated John Dear for the Nobel Peace Prize.

John Dear has been featured in the *New York Times*, the *Washington Post, USA Today, National Public Radio's "All Things Considered,"* and elsewhere. He is featured regularly on the national radio show "Democracy Now!" and in the *Huffington Post*. He is the subject of the DVD documentary "The Narrow Path" (with music by Joan Baez and Jackson Browne) and is profiled in *John Dear On Peace*, by Patti Normile

(St. Anthony Messenger Press, 2009). His nearly thirty books have been translated into ten languages. John Dear is on the staff of Pace e Bene and a priest of the Diocese of Monterey, California. Visit *www.johndear.org*.